# CELTIC WOMEN

# CELTIC WOMEN

## In Legend, Myth and History

LYN WEBSTER WILDE

Colour illustrations by Courtney Davis

BLANDFORD

*To my mother, the writer Jan Webster,*
*and to my grandmothers,*
*Daisy Webster and Margaret McCallum*

First published 1997 in the United Kingdom by
CASSELL PLC
Wellington House, 125 Strand, London WC2R 0BB

Distributed in the United States by Sterling Publishing Co., Inc.
387 Park Avenue South, New York, NY 10016–8810

**A Cataloguing-in-Publication Data entry for this title is available
from the British Library**

ISBN 0 7137 2552 4

Typeset by Keystroke, Jacaranda Lodge, Wolverhampton

Printed and bound in Spain by Bookprint S.L., Barcelona

Line drawings on pages 73, 74 and 75 by Craig Chapman.

# CONTENTS

# PREFACE

OUDICCA stands in a scythed chariot, her red hair flaming, urging her enraged people on against the invading Romans; Queen Maeve lolls languidly between battles, wondering which handsome warrior to take to bed next; pure-hearted St Brigit watches at the door of a woman in labour, ready to step in and help if things go wrong – these are the kinds of image that spring to mind when 'Celtic women' are mentioned. There is pride and strength here, and glamour, and sometimes a distinctive spiritual atmosphere which still has great power. But what is the reality behind these impressions? Were the lives of Celtic women much different from those of their Roman, Anglo-Saxon or Norse sisters? Was this a society where women could have authority, status and power, where they were generally viewed with respect, or one where they were denigrated, subjugated and suppressed?

I am going to try to answer these questions, but it is no easy task. There have been many different moments of 'Celtic Renaissance' in the past centuries, when people have delved back into the history of the Celtic lands, aiming to discover the truth about this intriguing culture, but usually ending up producing romantic fantasies which reflect the values of their own time. Our own age is no different: we would like the women of this past culture to be the kind of women we admire today – strong, independent, intuitive, loving and protective of the weak and yet ready to fight for what they believe in. We may dismiss evidence as distorted and unimportant if it does not fit in with what we want to see. The 'truth' varies depending on who is looking for it, and every writer about the Celts has a different point of view, ranging from the extremely fey and mystical through to the iconoclastically down to earth. This mass of material is like the brew in a great bubbling cauldron which tastes different every time you plunge your finger into it, depending on who has seasoned and stirred it last.

When we read the stories of Scathach, the woman teacher of warriors in the Cuchulain saga, or of beautiful Deirdre, who preferred to die rather than be humiliated by her lover's killers, or of Arianrhod, who fought to protect the women's mysteries against greedy, clever male magicians, we may feel our hearts beat faster as we come into contact with their magnificent spirits and think, 'Yes, these women possessed a power and an integrity which we have lost, and which we ought to find again.' But when we read about the mysterious graves where old women were buried, beheaded and face down,

6

*Boudicca, queen of the Iceni, with her two daughters.*
(Cardiff City Council)

with their weaving spindles laid beside them, or about the woman who was buried alive, bound to a much younger man who may have fathered the child whose miscarried body lay between her legs, we shiver with horror at this taste of ancient barbarism. We may decide that, then as now, women were suppressed and thwarted, and opt to forget the past and hope for a better future.

Maybe there is a middle way, somewhere between falling in love with our forebears, and thereby glamorizing them, and dismissing their lives as nasty and brutish. If we can carefully and patiently weave a web of all the threads from the past we can find – archaeological evidence, travellers' tales, folklore, incidents from the oldest versions of the stories – perhaps at the end of our labour, when we lay out the cloth, we will see appearing a new figure in the fabric, something both surprising and familiar which will give us an immediate, glancing glimpse of the reality of one or more Celtic women. We might, just for a moment, *know* them, and look at the world from inside their heads instead of our own. Of course, this could easily be an illusion, a reflection of ourselves, but that is a risk we have to take if we are curious.

The art of weaving is one of the oldest women's mysteries (although it was and is practised by men in some cultures) and perhaps the magic of that act will protect us from going too far wrong in our speculations. So that male readers do not feel left out, let us say that we will give them a temporary magical shield to protect them from the customary fate of men who sneak up to spy on a female mystery in action: being torn to pieces by the angry throng. Strong women need strong men, and in Celtic literature there are plenty of both. There is also plenty of evidence of the struggles between the sexes: take a look, for example, at the arguments between Queen Maeve and her husband, Ailill, in the *Tain Bo Cuailnge* (*The Cattle Raid of Cooley*), or Arianrhod and her brother Gwydion in *The Mabinogion*, or St Adamnan and his determined mother, Ronnat, in the early Christian records. In the battle of the sexes, though, the only winners are the products of that creative conflict, be they children, books, great ideas or whole cultures . . .

So that both male and female readers of this book will have the best chance of getting something useful from it, I have tried to present the facts as clearly as possible, and when I am speculating I have made that clear too, thus allowing you either to accept my interpretation or weave your own web from the threads gathered. We can give ourselves courage by remembering that the Celtic tradition is a living one, and that what we offer in our works and thoughts nourishes it at both root and branch – and changes it too.

I am, like many British (and Irish, Australian, New Zealand, European and North American) people, of at least partly Celtic origin. My mother's family, the McCallums, come from Argyllshire, the old Celtic kingdom of Dalriada. My father's family, the Websters ('Webster' means 'weaver' in

Anglo-Saxon), come from Glasgow and could therefore have originally been Angles, Saxons, Picts, Vikings, Normans or Celts, and perhaps, more likely, a complete mixture! I am going into this detail about my background only to make clear that although I love and respect the Celtic culture, I have equal respect for other races and cultures who have woven their threads into the fabric of life in these islands, and further afield. Celtic women were not alone in their glory: Viking women fought as warriors, the Anglo-Saxon women of the Dark Ages were a mighty force in the building of the Christian Church; and the Picts (who may or may not have been of Celtic origin) had the only attested matrilinear society in the British Isles.

# ACKNOWLEDGEMENTS

I owe a great debt to the indefatigable disputants of the Oxford Mysteries Group, with whom the different male and female definitions of virginity and other critical points have many times been beaten out, and an incalculable debt to the Man in the Kitchen, who tricked me into investigating all this in the first place. Gratitude is also due to members of the women's groups with whom I have experienced something of this tradition at first hand, and to my husband, Colin, who never lets me get away with anything.

I would like to thank Thomas Kinsella for allowing me to quote liberally from his translation of the *Tain* published by Oxford University Press, Macmillan for Yeats's 'A Prayer for My Daughter', Marion Campbell for the extracts from her novel *The Dark Twin* (Turnstone, 1973) and Nuala ni Dhomhnaill for verses from her *Pharaoh's Daughter* (Gallery Books, 1990).

Lastly, humble thanks to Courtney Davis and Craig Chapman whose outstanding illustrations truly embody and illuminate the spirit of Celtic women.

# SPELLINGS AND PRONUNCIATION

The spelling of Welsh, Gaelic and particularly Irish names can become a nightmare if you do not speak the languages; in just three books you can easily come across as many different versions of the same name! One might be the Anglicized form, one the ancient spelling and one the modernized version. Adding to the confusion is the fact that many of the vowels and consonants are not pronounced as in standard spoken English. I have decided to use the simplest versions wherever possible, usually Anglicized because this is the commonest usage (for example, 'Maeve' for the Irish 'Medb') and makes pronunciation easier.

Where I have used the Welsh, Gaelic or Irish spellings, this is because I have only ever come across the name used in its original form. So speakers of the Celtic languages, please forgive my pragmatism; but I feel it is more important that readers should enjoy the stories than worry about how to say the words or be 'linguistically correct'.

# THE CELTS –
# AN INTRODUCTION

A smoky glamour hangs about the Celts, and before we step into it, let us stand back and review the bare facts. The people we now call the Celts emerged into history around the year 500 BC, when they were spreading out from their homelands in Central Europe east towards Turkey and Greece, west towards the countries we now call Germany, France, Britain and Ireland, and south into Italy and Spain. They were a vigorous, warlike race, skilled in metalworking and horsemanship, and keen to trade. They had evolved a distinctive curvilinear artistic style which they used on both weapons and items of personal adornment. In the Celtic heartlands of Hallstatt in Austria and La Tène in Switzerland, rich graves containing chariots and golden jewellery have been found which show that this was a sophisticated society with strong links to the classical world. The main Celtic invasion of Britain and Ireland was thought to have taken place some time after 400 BC, although many scholars now believe that there may have been several earlier waves of Celtic immigrants who had already settled in Britain by this time.

If this is the case, it may be that in the Iron Age in Britain, Ireland and France we should imagine a society in which the incoming, iron-using warrior Celts ruled an established native population consisting partly of earlier waves of Celtic peoples plus groups of even earlier settlers whose origin is uncertain. This might explain the confusion about what the Celts actually looked like: some travellers claimed that they were tall, fair-skinned and fair-haired, while elsewhere we hear that the Celts were small and dark. These small, dark people may well have been the remnants of the very first people to live in these islands after the last Ice Age. At any rate, via domination or assimilation, the different groups came to share the Celtic culture and language, although this later split into two groupings, the 'P' Celtic languages spoken in Wales, Brittany and Cornwall, and the 'Q' Celtic languages spoken in Ireland, Gaelic Scotland and the Isle of Man.

*Romano-Celtic brooch showing curvilinear style from Silchester, Hampshire,* circa *third century* AD.
(Craig Chapman)

The Romans took over and occupied Celtic Gaul from the second century BC and reached southern England in AD 43. From here they spread into Scotland and Wales, although they never attempted to conquer Ireland and were soon pushed out of northern Scotland. From that time the indigenous Celtic culture was mixed with Roman customs and laws so that it was irrevocably changed. It was only in Ireland that a purely Celtic culture persisted until the Viking raids of the eighth century AD.

12

# A WARRIOR RACE

The Romans considered the Celts a savage and barbarous people, while admiring their courage and aggression and being intrigued by their alien traditions. Julius Caesar, who visited Gaul and Britain in the mid-first century BC, remarked in his *Gallic Wars* on their strange marriage customs: 'Wives are shared between groups of ten or 12 men, especially brothers, and between fathers and sons, but the offspring of these unions are counted as the children of the man with whom a particular woman cohabited first.' This may well have been a purely local arrangement, not one common to all Celtic lands!

He also marvelled at their extraordinary battle tactics: 'In chariot fighting the Britons begin by driving all over the field hurling javelins, and generally the terror inspired by the horses and the noise of the wheels are sufficient to throw the opponents' ranks into disorder.' Others were shocked by the Celtic habit of hacking off the heads of enemies defeated in battle and taking them home to bring them forth proudly as embalmed keepsakes at a later date.

Society was divided into three main groups: a spiritual and intellectual élite, consisting of druids, bards and prophets, who underwent a long period of training before they could practise; an aristocratic warrior class, from which were drawn the kings; and lastly the farmers, who tended the beasts and tilled the land. There were subsidiary classes, including craftsmen, entertainers and other sorts of skilled workers, and there were also slaves, taken as booty during raids. Warfare and raiding seem to have been a way of life. Caesar also records that the Celtic warriors had little fear of death because they believed in the transmigration of souls, and were therefore brave to the point of madness.

# THE CELTIC PEOPLES TODAY

During the late Iron Age in mainland Europe the Celts gradually merged with other racial groups and largely lost their separate identity. In Britain waves of Germanic settlers, the Angles, Saxons and Jutes who arrived in numbers after the Romans left, either conquered and assimilated the Celtic peoples, or pushed them westwards, into Wales, northwestern England, the Isle of Man, Cornwall and Scotland. Later the Scandinavian and Norman invaders poured in from all sides, diluting the Celtic culture still further. As already noted, Ireland was a purely Celtic country until the Viking raids of the eighth century AD and then the Norman invasion of the Middle Ages. In France, Brittany remained a Celtic enclave, and its culture was renewed when fleeing British–Celtic emigrants went there to settle during the German raids of the Dark Ages. Irish Celts sailed over to western Scotland in the sixth century AD and established the Gaelic kingdom of Dalriada in what is now Argyllshire.

All this means that while many English people will have Celtic blood, Celts will nowadays tend to be found in Ireland, parts of Scotland, Wales and northwestern England, the Isle of Man and Cornwall – and, of course, Brittany. Galicia in Spain still retains some Celtic identity and customs too. In addition, many Scottish and Irish Celts have been obliged either by English oppression (the clearances of the land so that big landlords could run them for profit) or economic necessity to emigrate to the New World – America, Canada, Australia, New Zealand.

But since no one can be sure where 'Celtic blood' actually came from in the first place, or which wave of Celtic invasion represents the 'real' Celts, no one can claim to be a 'pure' Celt – which is probably a good thing! In addition, some scholars are now suggesting that it is absurd to link together the people of La Tène in 400 BC with the Irish of the early Christian period under the label 'Celt'. Furthermore, they claim that the concept of 'the Celt'

*Grave of a noblewoman buried with krater at Vix, France, sixth century BC.*
(Craig Chapman)

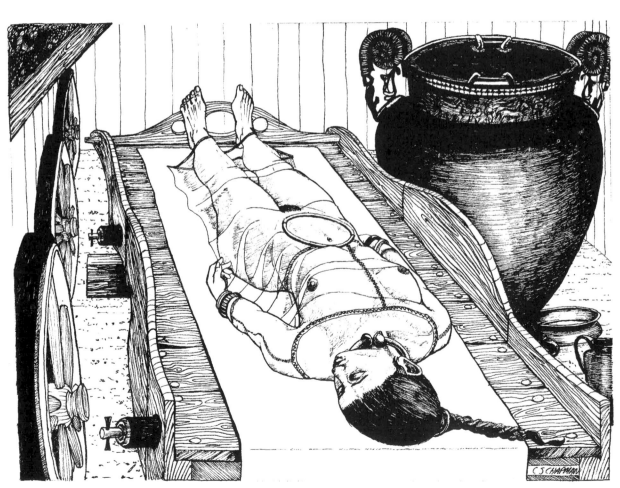

14

is something invented in the 1700s which has no objective reality. Whether or not this is true, the label 'Celt' does mean something important to many people now. It stands for a group of languages, stories, songs, a style of art, even a way of living your life which is different from the dominant 'Anglo-Saxon' mode. People who are 'Celts' by either birth or choice seem increasingly to want to protect their culture from the creeping 'Anglicization' of Great Britain and Ireland, or the 'Frankifying' of Brittany.

For the purposes of this book, we will be concentrating on the Celts who lived from around 400 BC up until the early Middle Ages, although in the last chapters we will see how the spirit of Celtic women has expressed itself right up to the present day. It is so easy to get general information about the Celts from the many good books available (see References) that I have decided to keep this sort of material to a minimum in order to leave maximum space for discussion of women and their experiences, about which there is much less to hand. In fact, there are many clues about the lives of Celtic women scattered about in archaeology and literature, but so far they have been drawn together mostly by men. When men write about women in myth and history they tend to indulge in extreme speculation and idealization which can be inspiring (consider Robert Graves's marvellous *The White Goddess*) but is rarely objective.

## OUR SOURCES OF INFORMATION

There are four main sources of information about Celtic women. The first is archaeology. Celtic graves and settlements have been found all over Europe. Modern techniques enable a great deal to be read from bones and pottery shards, and some very impressive items have been found intact too, such as the gigantic krater (vessel) in the grave of a rich and respected woman at Vix in France.

The second source is the written reports of travellers and soldiers from the classical world, such as Julius Caesar, Dio Cassius and Strabo. Sometimes these men may have been telling tall tales or misinterpreting what they saw, but on the other hand many of their accounts have the rough ring of truth about them.

The third source is the body of vernacular literature from Ireland and Wales which, although not written down until the tenth century at the earliest, is thought to contain tales passed on by oral tradition from much earlier, even as far back as the Iron Age. Because these stories were taken down by Christian scribes, you would expect some distortion, but in many cases there does not appear to be too much editing going on. There are also lives of saints and documents concerned with Irish Brehon laws which contain material relevant to women.

15

Most of this written material is Irish, which means that a disproportionate amount of evidence for the lives of women will seem to come from there, but because Ireland was never conquered by the Romans, it does give us a unique example of a society which remained purely Celtic for a long time.

In telling the stories I have stayed close to the oldest versions and on the whole have avoided the kind of interpretative psychologizing which can destroy the freshness and ambiguity of the stories (I have left the speculations for afterwards!). However, where possible I have told the stories from the woman's point of view, and when writing about real women such as Boudicca and Cartimandua I have allowed myself a little more freedom, in order, I hope, to make them come alive. Where there is a particularly good translation available, I may have used it in part or whole, provided I was able to obtain permission to do so.

The fourth source of material is folktales and traditions, either preserved in the work of collectors like W. Y. Evans Wentz or Alexander Carmichael or in some cases still part of people's lives.

## WOMEN IN A WARRIOR CULTURE

The people whom the Celts conquered and merged with as they swept into western Europe may well have once been goddess-worshipping hunter-gatherers, and indeed in the old Irish invasion myths in the *Lebor Gabala* there are passages which suggest this, but their own society certainly seems to have been dominated by what we now think of as 'male' values. The vast majority of characters in the Irish and Welsh stories are male; the culture they tell of is a warrior culture, where strength, skill at arms, fury and fierceness are the most valued attributes. Cuchulain is the hero of the *Tain*, not Maeve, the devious, warlike queen he is fighting. The restless, imaginative, questing Celts were not a matriarchal people. On the whole they were ruled by kings not queens, their druids and priests were usually male, and the fathers held sway in the households. In many other cultures of this period – for example, the Greek or the Scythian – we know that women led extremely circumscribed lives, completely subservient to the males, so why suppose that the Celts were any different?

It would be easy to collect all the instances of the abuse of women in the old tales and deduce from them that women had low status in the Celtic world: poor Macha, forced to run a race against the king's horses when about to give birth to twins; Queen Rhiannon turned into a beast of burden for a crime she did not commit; Deirdre raped by her lover's murderer. But this would be to apply a superficial analysis to multilayered material. Macha is terribly abused, but her revenge is terrible too: she puts a curse on the men of Ulster so that whenever they are needed in a moment of crisis, they will

16

be incapacitated by pains like the pains of a woman in labour. This surely is a measure of the kind of muscle the Irish Celts attributed to women. Maybe here we sense traces of the old goddess-worshippers, who knew that to insult the female powers was to transgress against the divine world they guarded and embodied, and indeed to pay a terrible price.

There are three other factors which seem to undermine this male hegemony. First, it has been remarked by several commentators that the most vivid, rounded and interesting characters in the Celtic stories, the ones who stick in your mind afterwards, are often female. Second, there are plenty of references in the literature to priestesses, queens, women warriors, druids, poets, prophets, healers and even lawyers, which seems to prove that women were not routinely excluded from holding positions of power in public life, even if the norm was for men to have them. And third, alongside and beyond the immediate world of fighting, feuding, wooing, betraying and conquering, there is presented another world, sometimes called 'the Otherworld', a hidden, inner world where women are the rulers.

Do not fall on a bed of sloth,
Let not thy intoxication overcome thee;
Begin a voyage across the clear sea,
If perchance thou mayst reach the land of women.[1]

In the society evoked by the old tales and verses, men rule the *outer* world, the world of achievement and action, the sunlit world of adventure and glory controlled by time, while women rule the *inner* world, the world of reflection, magic, transformation and regeneration, a world which is timeless, lit by the moon. At birth and death, where the worlds meet, it is women who are the guardians and ministers, whether as midwives or keeners at the graveside. The banshee, the Irish fairy woman whose bloodcurdling lament would be heard when someone was about to die, is a good example of this type of borderland being.

So it is likely, although we can never be sure, that Celtic women did indeed enjoy more freedom and respect than women in other lands during the Iron Age and early Christian era, because although the goddesses could be trampled and degraded (as Macha is by the men of Ulster) or challenged by male heroes (as Maeve is by Cuchulain), their power was never wiped out. It percolated instead into the Otherworld, from where it could nourish the fey women and half-goddesses who haunt the psyche of the Celtic peoples right up to the present day. You can still see it looking out of the eyes of partying hen-night girls in Belfast or Liverpool, emanating from the formidable bosoms and fierce eyes of Glasgow matriarchs, effervescing in the bold, mischievous sensuality of the female poets writing in Gaelic today, and celebrated in the new folk-based wave of Celtic women singers and musicians.

*'Islands of women',
hidden, inner worlds
ruled by women.*
(Michael J. Stead)

# 2 THE EVERYDAY LIFE OF A CELTIC WOMAN

A whole band of foreigners will be unable to cope with one of the Gauls in a fight, if he calls in his wife, stronger than he by far and with flashing eyes, least of all when she swells her neck and gnashes her teeth, and poising her huge white arms, begins to rain blows mingled with kicks, like shots discharged by the twisted cords of a catapult. The voices of most of them are formidable and threatening, alike when they are good-natured and angry. But all of them with equal care keep clean and neat, and in those districts, particularly in Aquitania, no man or woman can be seen, be she never so poor, in soiled or ragged clothing, as elsewhere.

When Ammianus Marcellinus wrote this in the fourth century AD, was he serious or was it a wry in-joke at the expense of the barbarous Celts and their unladylike women? Perhaps the most likely answer is that it is a humorous exaggeration with much truth in it: the Celtic women may well have been strong and good at fighting, but certainly not stronger than their warrior husbands. That they were clean and proud of their appearance we know from other sources, and the marvellous gold ornaments you can find in museums attest to their love of looking good. But we must remember that Ammianus was under the sway of a culture where women were absolutely excluded from the decision-making processes of life: Roman matrons stayed at home, had no political power (except that of pillow talk) and were always seen as belonging to a man, be it their father, their husband or another male relative. So we can imagine how shocking it was for Ammianus to contemplate a woman jumping up to defend her husband, and how he would cover his amazement with sneers.

From the reports of other Greek and Roman travellers and soldiers we know that the Celts did not expect women to be quiet and submissive, that women participated in battle using weapons of psychological warfare such as screeching and dancing and the pulling of faces. Other accounts show that the aristocratic women at least were assertive, ruthless and had a high opinion of their own worth, as is shown in the story opposite.

It would seem that Celtic women were not systematically confined – kept indoors like Greek women, or in wagons, so that their health suffered, like Scythian women – that they were felt to be partners to men and not their servants. Although most of the burials which have been excavated are male, there are also a good proportion of females, some interred with all

*Chiomara's Revenge*

**D**URING a battle between the Galatian Celts and the Romans, Chiomara was captured and raped by a centurion. When he discovered that she was an aristocrat he sent to her husband, Ortagion, and demanded a ransom for her release. It was arranged that the money would be handed over on the banks of a river, but while the centurion was counting his gold, Chiomara ordered that he be decapitated and afterwards presented his head to her husband, remarking that it was better that there should be only one man alive who'd had intercourse with her.[2]

signs of honour and wealth. At Vix, near Mont Lassois in France, a tomb was found dating from the end of the sixth century BC. In it lay a woman of about 35, her skeleton resting on the chassis of a chariot whose wheels were propped against the walls of the chamber. By her head was an exquisite golden torc, and filling the rest of the room were various drinking vessels, including a massive bronze krater, over 1.5 metres (5 feet) high, which was made in Sparta or Greek Italy. Apart from showing the trade links with the classical world which existed at this time, the grave certainly indicates that some women held high status. Whether this was the grave of a noble princess, queen or priestess who may have used the krater for sacrificial purposes (to be filled with human blood?), we do not know.[3]

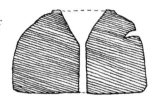

## HEALTH AND WELL-BEING

Life in the Iron Age and the early centuries of the Christian era was hard, and the struggle for survival was even fiercer for women than for men. Excavations in east Yorkshire suggest that life expectancy for women was much lower than for men: analysis of skeletal remains shows that if they survived childhood, most men would live into their twenties, thirties and early forties, whereas women would more commonly die in their teens or twenties, probably because of complications in childbirth. Women also suffered more osteoarthritis of the spine than men (perhaps caused by back-breaking work like turning the quernstones to mill flour and the dampness of their living quarters) and their teeth contained less calcium – breast-feeding would be the most likely cause.[3] Still, some women would live into middle and old age, either because they were strong or because they belonged to the aristocratic classes who would do less of the hard work and be better nourished and taken care of in childbirth. And, of course, those who lived in peaceful times with good harvests would have a much

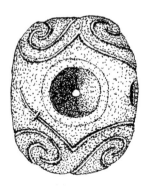

*Beehive rotary quern-stone from County Galway,* circa *first century BC.*
(Craig Chapman)

better quality of life than those living in war-torn times or in periods of shortage and hunger. And clearly the cultural life of a Celtic princess growing up in 600 BC in Hallstatt, Austria, would be utterly different from the experience of a Dark Age Irish nun witnessing the spread of Christianity in her land.

*Reconstruction of an Iron Age roundhouse, Castle Henlys, Dyfed, Wales.*
(Simant Bostock)

22

Before we meet individual Celtic women from history, myth and archaeology, we need to build up a sense of what the texture of their day-to-day lives would have been like, and, to avoid generalizing, we must choose a moment in time and place, hoping that it will be typical in most ways of the Celtic lifestyle. I have chosen a moment towards the end of the Iron Age in northern Britain. All the information used in what follows comes from reputable sources; only in characterization, timing and placing have I allowed myself a little leeway. For instance, some of the facts about dyeing come from the Ireland of an unspecified 'ancient' period; I have pushed them back a few centuries.

## THREE WOMEN OF THE BRIGANTES

Let us consider three women living in a settlement in northwestern England, in what we now call Cumbria, in the years just before Christ was born. They are part of a tribe which the Romans will call the Brigantes, but the Romans so far have merely visited and not invaded the land. The three women are Boann, an 18-year-old Irish slave with two small children; Calle, the matriarch of the household, still healthy in her late thirties, with four sons aged from 20 to six, one daughter and a number of foster children; and Scadi, aged 11, one of those foster children, sent to Calle by her mother, a priestess in Scotland, to be trained and looked after until she is old enough to marry or become a priestess herself. The head of the household is Marru,

*Reconstruction of an Iron Age settlement, Irish National Heritage Park, Wexford, Eire.* (Simant Bostock)

23

a druid in his early forties. They all live with the other members of their extended family, in a circular house about 15 metres (50 feet) across, supported on wooden poles, with wattle and daub walls and a steep thatched roof. In the centre a fire is kept burning more or less all of the time, with a couple of big cauldron pots hanging over it supported by firedogs, in which some sort of broth or stew is usually cooking. On the periphery of the house under the eaves are a number of stalls or cubicles in which straw and implements are stored and in which people – and sometimes animals – sleep. The entrance to the house is hung with big sheets of felt which are fixed back on warm days to let the light and air in, but in the winter kept closed to keep in the heat from the fire.[4]

## Boann the Slave

Boann and her two little boys sleep on straw in the stall next to the animals. When she was eight years old, she had been taken in a raid made by the Brigantes on a roving Irish tribe which had been harrying them. Her jobs are to mind and milk the cows, make butter and grind corn – all the heaviest labour. This is a 'civilized' household, being headed by a druid, so she is not mistreated and normally gets enough to eat and drink. However, she lives in dread of rape by the biggest foster sons, because although this is forbidden by Calle it does happen, and of being sold on to another family who might treat her less well. Along with cows, female slaves are used as units of currency and can be bought and sold without their consent. No one pities Boann, but when his foster children are cruel to her, Marru reminds them that if their fortunes changed, they too might be taken as slaves, and therefore recommends that they speak kindly to the girl.

## Calle the Mistress

Calle is a formidable woman, with fiery dark-auburn hair and the strong, sturdy arms and legs of a hill-dweller. She comes from the mountain regions of the northwest – what we now call the highlands of Scotland. Where she was born there are customs of matrilineal succession, so she is used to being treated with respect. She has the boys beaten if they misbehave towards women and is quite capable of doing it herself if Marru is not around. She spends a large part of her day either dyeing or weaving wool on her loom. Calle is much admired for her arts, having brought with her from the north the secrets of certain plants which no one else knows how to find and treat in order to obtain the necessary dyes. There is also a tiny whelk whose secretions produce the much-sought-after purple colour. Calle has found the best places on the coast to collect these, a secret which she takes care not to divulge. She also has the memory in her of the intricate checked patterns worn by her own people, so the cloth she produces is treasured and kept for best. Once the cloth is woven, Calle is much in demand as an overseer of the 'waulking' (shrinking, stretching and finishing) process, because she combines a good eye for what the cloth needs with a good memory for the best songs and stories which the women sing and tell while they work.

Apart from practising her arts, Calle must organize the household, making sure that good meats are boiled or spit-roasted for the feasts which she and her husband regularly give, good ale and mead brewed. Again, she has special recipes which she will rarely divulge. At the feasts themselves, she will sit back and let her foster children serve the food and drink while she enjoys listening to the tales. It is considered taboo for women to tell hero-tales, so Calle just listens, though among the women she is reckoned a wonderful 'spinner of yarns' (perhaps this phrase came into being from the fact that many stories were told while weaving and spinning were going on). Calle does not begrudge the bards their glory. After all, men are not allowed to watch women while they are engaged in the tricky processes of dyeing; if a man or boy does peek in, the whole batch of dye has to be thrown away, because they will have put the evil eye on it.[5]

At the feasts the favourite meat is wild boar that has been caught in the nearby forests (diminishing all the time as they are cleared by the expanding population), but folk are also offered mutton and beef, plus fish caught in the lakes or off the coast. Bread will be served with meals, along with ale and mead sweetened with honey. We know the Celts also had vegetables such as celery, beans and peas, and herbs such as wild garlic and chives, so their food may have been quite tasty. According to Roman reports, they sat on the floor and ate with their hands, using knives to fillet out tasty morsels, but were clean in their table manners and fond of their drink. Calle has many a time stepped in to humour a drunken warrior out of the idea of engaging in combat during a meal; apart from the noise and general upset, she does not like to have the sheepskins spread around the fire stained with blood.

## Scadi the Foster Child

As for Scadi, she is considered most fortunate to be fostered in such an accomplished family. While Marru's brother, Temir, trains the boys in the arts of war, and Marru himself teaches the clever ones the druidic lore, Calle passes on to Scadi what she can of the women's mysteries. Apart from the secrets of dyeing and weaving and waulking, there is much to learn about conception and birth. Scadi is getting to the age when she will start to bleed and needs to be told about the laws of the moon – when she could conceive if she lay with a boy and when she would probably be safe to enjoy herself without fear. Later Calle might impart to her certain recipes for causing the abortion of an unwanted baby, and others for drinks and salves useful to women in childbed. It is gossiped about in the locality that Calle mysteriously stopped conceiving in her mid-thirties, and most of the women think she knows which substances to take in order to stop a baby taking hold in the womb. About this secret Calle is completely silent: she knows that the men, even wise Marru, would not approve of women having such control over their own fertility, but she is determined to live long enough to pass on her wisdom, not merely reproduce herself.

Calle does not specialize in healing, but if Scadi showed an aptitude she might be sent off to a group of three unmarried sisters living in the forest who are renowned for their special knowledge of herbs. If she turned out to be a very gifted child, then Marru himself might impart to her some of the knowledge that can be passed on only across the sexes, man to woman or woman to man. This would include an understanding of the calendar: which days are good for sowing seed or starting an enterprise and which are not, and how to predict on what day the shortest and longest days of the year will fall. Then again, she might be considered as a candidate for training as a priestess, possibly in the shrine of Brig, the 'Exalted One', after whom the tribe is named.

## Clothing

The weather at this time in Britain is very similar to today, which means it is often cold and wet. All three women wear a basic woven tunic, easily unfastened at the shoulders for breast-feeding, tied with a belt and with a cloak or shawl over the shoulders in cold weather. Calle is able to adorn her clothes with fine brooches made of gold and precious stones, to put golden lock-rings in her long dark hair and a golden torc around her neck. She wears leather shoes and her tunics or wraparound skirts are woven in bright checks and stripes. Boann must wear plainer cloth and often goes barefoot, but she too has an anklet and a bracelet of black shale, given her as love tokens by the fathers of her children. Scadi is a tomboy who so far does not bother with such things, though she has been known to experiment with dyeing her eyebrows black with berry juice and reddening her cheeks with elder.[5]

## Social Structure

This is a large and rich household, including not just Marru and Calle, their children, foster children and slaves, but also the families and slaves of Marru's two warrior brothers. In the land immediately outside the house there are storage pits for grain, raised huts for storing other foods safe from predators and damp, plots for herbs, a pen for a favourite cow and sheep, and a noisy guard dog tied to a post. At the perimeter a wicker fence and a deep ditch provide protection from marauding wolves or bears, and stop valuable animals escaping.[4] Living close by are the craftsmen, woodworkers,

*Woman in Iron Age Celtic dress.*
(Craig Chapman)

smiths and metalworkers who make weapons like shields and swords, farming implements and jewellery. There are craftswomen too – the three unmarried sisters mentioned already, for example, who not only possess the secret lore of plants, which enables them to heal or salve wounds, but also make pots for all the tribe.

## The Fire Festivals

Hospitality is an obligation of nobility, so on many evenings the household must entertain in their roundhouse, which is transformed into a scene of revelry. Even at ordinary feasts there will be bards and musicians telling the stories of family and tribe, but at the great fire festivals, which happen four times a year, the atmosphere is even more intoxicating. Everyone, from lowly Boann, with her squalling, bare-bottomed toddlers, to the awesome, aged Ana, Calle's mother-in-law, looks forward to these times, when the turning points in the year are celebrated. On the occasion of the feast of Beltane in early summer, the extended family will travel a day's walk away to the stronghold of their local chieftain, sleeping out overnight to be ready to climb the hill before dawn and see the ceremonial lighting of the great fire.

At home the hearth-fires will have been extinguished and for weeks beforehand the young people of the district will have been out gathering wood to make the fire, which must be built of nine sacred woods only, including alder, oak, hawthorn and hazel. There is a taboo against speaking the names of these woods in the period leading up to the festival. Then, as the sky becomes pearly with pre-dawn light, the people wait silently for the Lord of Light to rise up above the horizon and unite himself with the Lady, knowing that through their embrace abundance will be born. At the moment of their union the new fire is lit and a great shout goes up from the people. Then the sacrificial victims are slain (in this time bullocks but in the olden days, so Marru tells Scadi, it would have been human beings) and the preparation of the feast begins: plenty of milk, honey, oaten bannocks, juicy roasted meat, all washed down with ale and mead, and dancing, and soon many couples, not all of them in the first flush of youth, head off to the woods to make the beast with two backs.[6]

Calle no longer joins in. She knows another child at her age could kill her, and two of her sons were conceived at Beltane, by a secret admirer from the neighbouring settlement. Marru guesses that this is the case, but he does not mind. He understands that new blood in the family may bring in new talent and strength, and indeed one of his 'sons' looks like following him into the druid priesthood. Calle watches Boann carefully. She thinks two little bastards are quite enough to support and if the girl gives birth again, the child might have to be offered to the waves or left out in the wild – not something Calle likes to do, even with a slave child. But it is difficult to calm the blood on a summer's day when the ecstasy of sexual union is

*Owl goddess bracelet.*
(Craig Chapman)

27

heightened by the smell of blossom and the fire of ale in the belly, and some of the young warriors are so beautiful to look at, their hair stiff and bright with lime, standing up from their brows like coxcombs, the whirling undulating tattoos on their strong arms and backs . . . Boann slips away and Calle reflects that she may have to make some of her special mixture for the feckless girl to drink down in a couple of weeks.

Meanwhile, Scadi runs around crazily, overexcited like all the children, tumbling with the boys, singing rude songs to the more maidenly little girls to shock them. 'This will have to stop soon,' thinks Calle, 'or she'll be getting into trouble too.' Scadi is clever and alert but wayward, not necessarily the best combination for a priestess who must dedicate herself to the service of the Goddess for life.

The other major feast of the year is Samhain, when the stock must be slaughtered and preserved for the winter. Then the dead draw close to the living and you may converse with them if you will, asking questions and receiving answers. It is a feast of roasted meat and apples, and the official beginning of the season of storytelling. It being too cold to go off lovemaking in the woods, everyone gathers round the fire to hear the hero-tales, which must not be told during the day or in the light.

Other festivals are also celebrated in a humbler way. When the first ewes give milk, it is a sign that Brig's day has arrived, Brig the Goddess of the moon and of fertility. Boann has told them that over the sea in her land there is a special home for the Goddess where nine virgin priestesses tend a sacred flame, which must never be allowed to go out, a flame which no man must ever see.

In the late summer the harvest is celebrated with a feast sacred to Lleu, and this is the time when some young men and women choose a partner for the year ahead, to test out if they get on well enough together to make a permanent union.[6]

## War and Peace

Months and years can pass without major incident – perhaps skirmishes with neighbouring tribes, when cattle are stolen and revenge is sought, or feuds between individuals or bands of young men, but nothing serious in which women or children could be harmed. But then the tribes from across the sea or from beyond the northern hills will feel the need to expand and will start raiding again. Then no one will sleep without a watchman on the gate to keep an eye on the nearest high point, where a beacon will be lit if there is danger. And if the beacon is lit, the whole extended family will grab warm clothes and what food they can carry and hurry to the nearest hillfort, where they have a chance of defending themselves against the enemy, who would, of course, if they won, slaughter the men and take the able-bodied women and children prisoner. To be a slave in an alien land is every woman's

*Scottish sword, a symbol of the warrior's power, early sixteenth century.*
(British Museum)

28

nightmare, forced perhaps to be the abused concubine of some evil-smelling lordling if you still had your looks, raped and worked to death if you were plain or older, or, worst of all, sacrificed to alien gods.

Some women, like Calle, have decided they would rather die than suffer such humiliation and therefore keep the necessary poison to hand. For Boann, a change of ownership might make life even harder and she worries for her children, who have a chance of growing up free if they show valour in Marru's house but in a new place would surely be made slaves too. Scadi, at 11, has nightmares about it, and dreams of becoming a warrior woman so that she can cut off the heads of the bandits and stick them on poles above the porch.

## THE COMING OF THE ROMANS

In the second century BC the Romans invaded Gaul, and in AD 43 Britain, although they never conquered the north of Scotland or Ireland. They brought classical civilization and central heating to these barbarian shores and offered both men and women a different ideal of how to live their lives. Roman women were slightly better off than Greek women in that they were permitted to go out on their own to do shopping and to eat with their husbands rather than separately, and they could aim to be admired for their dignity and wisdom, but they certainly did not have the freedom of expression of the Celtic women.

*Coventina, a Romano-Celtic water goddess.*
*(Craig Chapman)*

29

It seems that the Roman and Romanized women looked down on their 'native' sisters, calling them '*welisc*' ('*welsh*' meaning 'foreign'), and in the cities at least, over the 400 years of Roman rule, many Celts were absorbed into the Roman way of life and lost to some extent their cultural identity. Nevertheless, some Celtic gods and goddesses survived, either under their own or under Roman names, and although they destroyed the druid stronghold of Anglesey in AD 60 the Romans did not otherwise interfere with the people's freedom of religion.

## CELTIC WOMEN IN CHRISTIAN TIMES

Christianity was established in Ireland by St Patrick in the fifth century AD and various spiritually gifted women such as Brigit, Ite and Monnenna were converted and established religious houses, some of them for women only, some for both sexes. They were hampered by unfair laws of inheritance, which meant that although they could own land while they lived, they could not pass it on to their own religious foundations when they died. However, for a long period, perhaps up until the Norman conquest of Ireland, women were respected as spiritual leaders and advisers of *both sexes* within the Church. There were religious establishments where monks and nuns were trained and worshipped alongside each other, but as the power of the Celtic Church was eroded by the champions of the Roman practices, women gradually lost this status and with it the chance to participate actively in the development of Christianity. We will be considering Celtic Christianity in more detail in Chapter 5.

### The Enigma of Adamnan and His Mother

For some women conditions of life in seventh-century Ireland were frankly gruesome, as this extract from the 'Law of Adamnan' makes clear.

> . . . and this was the *cumalach*, a woman for whom a hole was dug at the end of the door so that it came over her nakedness. The end of the meat spit was placed upon her till the cooking of the portions was ended. After she had come out of that earth-pit she had to dip a candle four men's hands in length in a plate of butter or lard; that candle to be on her palm until division of food and distribution of liquor and making of beds in the houses of kings and chieftains had ended.[1]

Adamnan was a seventh-century saint who was, so the story goes, tortured and blackmailed by his mother, Ronnat, into creating laws which would protect women and children from the dreadful abuses to which they were subject at the time. Adamnan's mother took him to a battlefield, and perched on his back as they picked their way through terrible scenes of carnage. They

*Ronnat, Adamnan's mother, urges him to obtain justice for Irish women.*

## How Ronnat Won Justice for Women

S THEY wandered the battlefield, gazing in horror at the mutilated bodies of the dead women, Ronnat turned and spoke to her son.

'Why don't you use the power of your priesthood to raise one of these poor women from the dead? Let's see what she has to say about her wretched life and death.'

Adamnan did as he was told and raised Smirgat, a royal woman from Tara. Immediately she spoke.

'Adamnan! I put you under a holy obligation to free the women of the western world. And I say that neither food nor drink shall go into your mouth until you have done the job.'

'How can I not eat?' protested Adamnan. 'If food or drink is set in front of me, then I'll take it.'

'We'll see about that!' said his mother, and she put a chain around his neck and a flintstone in his mouth so that he would have little choice but to obey.

When she returned to see him eight months later, Adamnan was covered with seagull's droppings from head to toe and scorched by salt water, but still his prayers for the freeing of women had not been answered. His mother was sorry for him but far sorrier for the women of Ireland, so she only softened as far as to change his torture: now she put him into a stone chest, with worms devouring his tongue and the slime of his brain seeping out of his ears.

After several years of intense prayer an angel appeared and told Adamnan that he could arise and leave the chest because women would be freed for him.

But the kings had other ideas. When he went to them to negotiate the freeing, they said: 'If it is done it will be over our dead bodies! Why should we want to allow women to disturb men's sleep, to have men fight and die rather than women? Let females be kept in bondage where they belong until the brink of Doom!'

But Adamnan was adamant. He wandered about with only his little altar bell for protection, ringing it and making dark pronouncements, threatening the kings that, unless they yielded, some of them would not succeed to the kingship of their fathers, others would leave no children to inherit their crowns, or their present sons would die of plague or accident. The kings wanted to kill him but the power of his holy bell was so great that eventually they gave in and promised that from henceforth anyone who injured, killed or interfered with women would be severely punished. Thus was the 'Law of Adamnan' born.

saw a little baby clinging to the headless corpse of its mother, a stream of milk upon one of its cheeks, a stream of blood on the other. The implication was that men were forcing their women to fight, 'flogging them to battle' in fact.

We do not know what literal truth there is in the tale of Ronnat (opposite), or how widespread was the cruelty it describes. It sounds as if we are talking here mainly of the harsh treatment of slave women, hostages taken in war, but a royal woman is mentioned too, as if making the point that no woman, however noble, was safe from the cruelty of men. The images evoked in the tale give us an insight into the ugly and brutal side of Celtic life: a warrior society seldom shows pity for the weak and the defeated, and the enjoyment of warfare can easily turn into bloodlust and sadism. In the grim description of women's sufferings there is a hint of a society which has lost its ethical basis and become decadent.

It is significant that the driving force behind the new law is not the Christian Adamnan, but his mother, Ronnat, who embodies the fierceness and determination of a powerful woman as yet untamed by Christianity. However, she recognizes that she must work through the new male-dominated religion if she is to stop women from being utterly crushed. The Christianizing of Ireland eventually brought to an end the practice of slavery. Unfortunately, while 'protecting' women from abuse, the Christian saints also managed to leech the power from their veins, relegating the Goddess to the subsidiary role of mother or midwife of Christ, in the persons of Mary and Brigit.

However, if we look behind the serene, idealized faces of the Virgin Mary and St Brigit, we find the beginnings of a secret trail which will lead us eventually to the shrine of the old Goddess, still glowing with all her barbarous power, beauty and dignity.

# 3 SEX, LOVE AND MOTHERHOOD

One day, during the Roman occupation of Britain, a Roman lady and the wife of a Caledonian chief were chatting. The Roman matron expressed herself surprised at the promiscuity of the Caledonian women. 'Well,' replied her companion, 'we find it much better to give ourselves openly to the best men, rather than let ourselves be debauched in secret by the vilest, as you Romans do!'[8] We can imagine the look on the Roman woman's face. My own Scottish grandmother was equally conversant with the ancient Gaelic art of the sharp put-down.

This conversation was overheard by Dio Cassius in the third century AD, and it is thought to be the case that the Caledonians (a tribe of the Picts, who may have been at least partly Celtic and who certainly influenced the Celts) practised some form of polyandry – that is, they were entitled to have sexual partners apart from their official husbands. Caesar himself, visiting Britain three centuries earlier, wrote that the Celts practised a kind of communal marriage, where a woman might sleep with any of a family of brothers, though children would be held to belong to the man she first paired with. Other classical writers claimed to have noticed that incest and homosexuality were commonly practised in some Celtic communities. It may be that the Celts were much more lax in their sexual mores than the Romans, or the Roman writers may have been reacting to what were simply local anomalies. A third possibility is that the Romans made up tall stories to entertain people back home. It is very difficult for us today to disentangle the truth about these matters, partly because of lack of clear evidence, partly because we are so conditioned to view sexuality through the spectacles of a Christian culture which promotes monogamy and the sanctity of the nuclear family. How did Celtic women experience their sexuality? Were they much freer and more open in their expression of it, or did notions of restriction of desire and loyalty to one partner play a part too?

There are two factors we can be sure of. First, Celtic women lived far more *in their bodies* than we do, and in close contact with other bodies. Desire would have been a much more immediate sensation for them, easier to experience and to satisfy in a community where people lived in close physical proximity. However, there may have been fierce taboos against having sex with certain categories of people. A grave has been found at Garton Slack in east Yorkshire, in which a woman of about 30 and a much younger man were buried alive, with a post driven between them, pinning

34

their arms together. The remains of a miscarried foetus lay between the woman's legs, having been expelled while she was unconscious. It could be that the burial alive was a punishment for the transgression of some taboo. Was the woman a high-ranking noble who slept with a slave? Was the young man her nephew, or even her son? Or was it simply that she had disgraced her husband by getting pregnant by a young neighbour while he was away fighting?

Second, from their early teens onwards most women would have been either pregnant or breast-feeding, and suffering from the nutritional depletion that these can bring on, *unless* there were forms of contraception available (see later in chapter). Therefore the periods in which they would have had the energy to feel desire and enjoy sex could have been fairly limited.

Of course, this would depend on their socio-economic status. Doubtless the chieftain's wife mentioned above and her friends were more likely to have time and energy on their hands for lovemaking than slaves and poorer women. And it would be wrong to imply that the love lives of Celtic women were instinct-driven and without refinement, depth and courtly values. The Irish tales in particular reveal a culture in which both male and female beauty were relished, both male and female desire acknowledged, and the awesome and disruptive power of romantic love explored with understanding.

For an insight into the Irish Celtic attitudes to desire and romantic love, the story of Deirdre from the preamble narratives to the *Tain Bo Cuailnge* (*The Cattle Raid of Cooley*) is the best introduction. It is a tale from the eighth or ninth century AD and I have used Thomas Kinsella's excellent translation as the basis of this version (below). The fragment of song is left in the poet Kinsella's own words.[9] The word *geis* which crops up in the tale several times is not easily translated — here it means a sacred obligation which cannot be refused or denied.

## *Deirdre and the Sons of Uisliu*

**t**HE WOMAN groaned and leant up against the table to ease her back. The baby nearly due was wriggling and kicking in her womb. She wished her husband's drunken friends would stop their wiseacring and roaring. Hadn't she run around all night serving them meat and drink? Wasn't it time for her to go to her bed?

It was with relief that she heard them saying their goodnights, and so she straightened up and began to make her way to bed. But as she crossed the floor she felt a lurch in her womb and a ghastly, piercing, screeching scream came from it. She clutched her belly and screamed herself.

Alarmed, the men shouted to her to come to them, and her husband, Fedlimid, King Conchobar's storyteller, asked her what the uncanny noise was. She turned instinctively to Cathbad the druid, a wise man who always spoke the truth, however unpalatable.

'Cathbad, what is the meaning of this? Such a strange, horrible sound! Is my baby going to be all right?'

Cathbad put his hand on her belly. The baby kicked but did not scream again. He sighed.

'This little girl is going to bring misery and bloodshed to the men of Ulster,' he said gravely. 'Twining yellow hair, green-irised eyes, cheeks red as if a foxglove brushed them . . . She'll be beautiful, but unlucky and a bringer of evil to others too.'

It is not surprising that when the girl baby, named Deirdre, was born, the warriors of Conchobar's court felt that the child who would bring such suffering should be immediately destroyed.

'No, no,' said King Conchobar. 'She is going to be beautiful. I will have her reared especially for me.'

And so it was that Deirdre spent all her childhood in a secret, secluded place with only her foster parents for company – and the troublemaking satirist Leborcham, who could never be kept away.

One winter's day, when Deirdre had grown up to the brink of womanhood, she stood watching while her foster father was skinning a calf for her dinner. A raven hopped about on the snow drinking up the blood.

'You know,' she said to Leborcham dreamily, 'if I could meet a man with hair like that raven, skin the colour of that snow and cheeks the colour of that blood . . . '

'You won't have to look far to find him,' said Leborcham silkily. 'Such a man is Noisiu, son of Uisliu, and what's more you can easily meet him – he's not far off at this moment at all.'

Curious to see this beautiful man, Deirdre slipped away to the ramparts of the fort of Emain, where she heard Noisiu before she saw him. He was chanting to himself, unaware that anyone else was nearby. She listened, holding her breath. His singing was magical; cows gave more milk when they heard it and people were filled with peace. Soon she was enchanted too.

She could not resist going to meet him. He stopped singing and said, 'That's a fine heifer that's passing me today.'

'Heifers always grow fat when there are no bullocks around to give them exercise,' she riposted.

Noisiu laughed. He liked her quick wit. This must be the famously beautiful Deirdre, and yes, she was exquisite. What a shame she was already promised to the king!

'Well, you've got the finest bull of all lined up for you,' he said.

'But I'd much rather have a fine young bullock like yourself,' she replied. As soon as the jesting words were out of her mouth, she realized she meant them in earnest: he was the most lovely young man she had ever seen and she wanted him.

'That's not possible,' he muttered, 'you know it's not.'

'I know nothing,' she answered boldly, 'except that I shall take you by the ears and put a *geis* on you to take me away tonight.'

And she stepped towards him and took hold of his ears. Gently but firmly. At her touch he gasped, and flushed. Deirdre could feel the pulsing of the hot blood in his arms and waited for him to pull her to him.

Instead he screamed out loud for his brothers. When they came running, he told them that they must prepare to leave immediately with himself and Deirdre, before the king noticed their absence and hers.

'But why?' they asked. 'This would be a disastrous act which could ruin our lives.'

'I know,' spoke Noisiu, 'but I have no choice. We will be shamed if we do not fulfil the *geis* that Deirdre has laid on me.'

They understood. A life without honour was not worth living. That night the four of them ran away together with their warrior band.

So it was that after spending months as outlaws in Ireland, sleeping rough in the woods, surviving on poached game and tickled salmon, ever on the alert for the approach of Conchobar's men, they took a ship over to Scotland, which was called Alba then, and ended up serving the king there. He found out about Deirdre and her exceptional beauty even though the brothers kept her hidden, and sent a servant to try to lure her away. But she would not go. She was not even tempted. She loved Noisiu absolutely, and his brothers dearly. Although their life was dangerous and lonely, she never for a moment regretted putting a *geis* on Noisiu the day they met. But the king of Alba's devious efforts to get them killed in battle so that he could take Deirdre made their lives unbearable and they decided to return home to Ireland. A messenger came from King Conchobar saying that he had forgiven them and wanted to make peace.

'Thanks be to the Exalted One,' breathed Deirdre. 'But are we safe? Or is this a trick to catch us?'

'The king will send his best man, Fergus, to escort you. His presence will guarantee your lives.'

This news much reassured them, because Fergus was a man with the light of truth in his eyes. They knew that he would not betray them.

But once landed in Ireland, Fergus was waylaid at the house of a comrade who insisted that he stay with them for a night or two, and the laws of hospitality gave him no choice but to yield. Deirdre and the three sons of Uisliu proceeded without him to King Conchobar's court in Ulster. Deirdre was filled with foreboding, and her dreams were filled with blood, but it was too late to turn back.

As they walked into Conchobar's hall to meet the king, the three comely young warriors and the radiant Deirdre, a man called Eogan stepped forward to welcome Noisiu. He made as if to embrace the young man, but instead sank the blade of his spear deep into Noisiu's chest and then passed him over to Fergus's son, who flung himself like a dog on to the young man to finish him off. Noisiu's brothers had entered unarmed but fury gave them the strength to grab weapons from the onlookers and kill a handful of Conchobar's men before being overcome and killed themselves.

Deirdre stood stiffly watching. Then her hands were bound behind her back and she was led or rather pushed over to Conchobar's side. He turned her head to force her to look into his eyes, but she stared straight through him and nothing could make her focus on him. Later on he forced her to sleep with him, but her body was as lifeless as a puppet's. There was little pleasure in it for him except the satisfaction of conquest.

When Fergus heard about the slaughter, he gathered together some men and came and took revenge on the men of Ulster. Young women were slaughtered too, and the dreadful reverberations of Conchobar's betrayal echoed on for 16 years in Ireland, causing death, exile and misery in abundance. Meanwhile, the king tried to win Deirdre over, but she would not be moved. Neither would she eat or sleep or look after herself, although she did sing from time to time eerie little songs about her life in the wilds with Noisiu and his brothers.

'His cropped gold fleece I loved
and fine form – a tall tree.
Alas, I needn't watch today
nor wait for the sons of Uisliu.

I loved the modest, mighty warrior,
loved his fitting, firm desire,
loved him at daybreak as he dressed
by the margin of the forest.

Those blue eyes that melted women,
and menaced enemies, I loved;
then, with our forest journey done,
his chanting through the dark woods.

I don't sleep now,
nor redden my fingernails.
What have I to do with welcomes?
The son of Indel will not come.'

One day in exasperation Conchobar asked her, 'Whom do you hate the most in the world?'

*Deirdre, who preferred to die rather than be humiliated by her lover's killers.*

39

'You of course, and Eogan,' she replied. He was the man who had murdered Noisiu.

'In that case,' responded Conchobar, 'I shall give you to Eogan for a year.'

The next day Deirdre was seated in a chariot in front of Eogan and Conchobar. The king was taking her out to show off her humiliation to the people.

'Well, Deirdre,' he said, leaning forward to whisper in her ear, as the swift chariot bumped along on the rough ground, 'now you can eye us both just like a ewe between two rams!'

But Deirdre had sworn she would never belong to two men. As the chariot lurched round a corner, she leant out of it so that her head struck a passing rock hard and shattered. Her blood and brains spattered over the two men behind her as the chariot careened to a panicking halt.

Deirdre's fate is terrible, but she suffers it only after she has had what she wanted – Noisiu. Romantic love has triumphed over tyranny and lust. No one could hear the tale and be on Conchobar's side. Somehow Deirdre's dramatic death feels like a victory.

The story suggests that this was a society which would have liked the values of the male warriors to be paramount, so that a man's loyalty to his king or master would never be in doubt, but knew very well that the power of female desire made that impossible. It is Deirdre who chooses Noisiu and the *geis* which she lays on him binds him inescapably to her, just as that of Grainne binds Diarmaid in a later tale. Thousands of people die because she asserts her right to have the man she wants. The songs of love and longing which she sings when she has lost her lover (which may be a somewhat later addition to the text) vividly express the joy and pain of sexual love in its most poignant and refined form. Some scholars feel that the seeds of the traditions of courtly love, which flowered much later in the troubadours' tales and the Arthurian legends, are to be found in these early Irish stories. Certainly contemporary Anglo-Saxon works, although very fine indeed, do not address themselves to themes of romantic love and its associated agonies.

Deirdre is a tragic heroine, a passionate full-blooded woman who stakes all for love. That her choice of lover is an irresponsible act does not take away from our sympathy for her. Queen Maeve, however, is more of an anti-heroine. In the *Tain* she is presented as aggressive, argumentative and treacherous, with an enormous sexual appetite which can never be satisfied by one man: 'I never had one man without another waiting in his shadow,' she says.

Good as her word, she betrays her husband, Ailill, with his best friend, Fergus, and feels not a whit of guilt about it. Towards the end of the story her period starts just before battle is to be entered and the blood digs out three great channels, 'each big enough to take a household'.

We will be considering the figure of Maeve in detail later, but for now it is enough to say that her ebullient and unashamed sexuality is certainly meant to be enjoyed by those who hear or read the story. She is a firm link back to the time when women's sexuality was not treated as disgusting or unmentionable or non-existent – as shown in the story of Debforgaill below.

It is a gruesome tale, but it gives an intriguing insight into how the Irish Celts visualized female sexuality: the size of a woman's bladder, her *inner space*, seems to stand here for her sexual capacity, or perhaps her ability to give sexual pleasure because of the strength of her internal muscles!

On a much lighter note, when Alexander Carmichael was collecting the folk customs of the Highlands in the second half of the nineteenth century, he came across a tradition practised at the feast of Michaelmas, at the end of September, which is surely a throwback to the time before Christianity frowned upon female forwardness in sexual matters. On the eve of the feast the young women in the Western Isles would go with their friends to dig up wild carrots, being particularly delighted if they came across forked ones.

> Dear little forked one! Little forked one!
> Carrot joy unstinting to me!
> Dear little forked one! Little forked one!
> Carrot fulfilment unstinting to me![11]

That night at the dancing they would give their carrots to the men they fancied – as an invitation to indulge in the pleasures of fruitfulness sooner or later! In this culture, then, a woman had at least one chance a year to pick the man she wanted rather than be picked. And you can't get a clearer phallic symbol than a carrot!

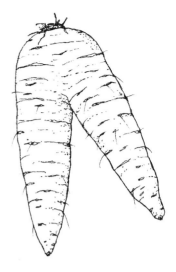

*Forked carrot, symbolic gift from Hebridean women to the men they desired.*
(Craig Chapman)

## The Death of Debforgaill

**f**OR SPORT one winter a group of women decided to have a urinating competition to see who could pee furthest onto the snow. Debforgaill, wife of King Lugaidh, was reluctant to play but agreed to do so in the end, and easily won. The other women were very jealous of her, saying that if the men knew about her talent they would desire only her and become dissatisfied with their own wives. So they tore out her eyes, cut off her nose, ears and hair, intending to put an end to her attractiveness. When Lugaidh returned, he found her at the point of death and killed himself in a fit of shock and despair. Cuchulain, who was with him at the time, overturned the house on top of the women responsible for the outrage, thus killing them too.[10]

# MARRIAGE LAWS

Caesar reports in his *Gallic Wars* that in Celtic Gaul the men had the power of life and death over their wives and children, but he also observes that women did have an equal right with men to inherit their shared wealth. In the Roman culture, on her husband's death a woman might find herself having to live with her father or son or brother, because she had no right to inherit the family home or wealth. Anglo-Saxon women were treated as chattels by their men, and there are graves in Britain where the twisted skeletons show that the women in them were alive when they were buried – to accompany their dead lords and masters to the land of the dead. Compared with their Greek or Roman or Anglo-Saxon sisters, British Celts certainly seem to have had more rights and more independence. The Irish Brehon laws gave free women, as opposed to slaves, social and property rights on a par with men. Husband and wife continued to own the respective shares they brought into the marriage, such as land, flocks and household goods, so that if they divorced they would each take away their own part. Divorce was permitted on either side. A woman was responsible for her own debts and not those of her husband.[5]

However, there were unfair anomalies: a father could give evidence against his daughter in a Brehon's court, but she was not permitted to refute it by her evidence. A woman was supposed to be given a fair share of her husband's property on his death, but this part of the law was not always enforced. If the fierce pirate Grace O'Malley (see Chapter 8) could not get her rights in this respect, then there must also have been many weaker women who did not get theirs. A picture emerges, in fact, of a patriarchal culture which was fair to women if those women had wealth and/or power of some sort. This is echoed by the customs of naming and of noting lineage: normally a son would be named after his father, as in 'Noisiu son of Uisliu'. However, where the mother was an important woman, the son might take her name, as in 'Conchobar mac Nesa', 'Conchobar son of Nes', where Nes is a female character in the preamble tales of the *Tain*. And Tacitus is pointing to the same kind of sexual pragmatism when he writes, 'In Britain there is no rule of distinction to exclude the female line from the throne, or the command of armies.' What this means is that while kings and commanders were almost always male, there was no objection to a woman doing the job if circumstances or her temperament demanded it – Queens Boudicca, Cartimandua and Maeve are the classic examples.

Usually in Ireland men had just the one wife, although concubinage was allowed also, and presumably, since the concubines could be slaves, they did not have the legal rights and protections which wives enjoyed. But there was also a custom in Ireland and in Scotland (where it lasted until the Middle Ages if not longer) of trial marriage. In Scotland these year-long partnerships would be entered into at the harvest festival of Lammas, and if they did not work out well could be dissolved the following Lammas, with any child which had been produced going to the father. We might interpret this as unfair to the woman, but in a society which was much less sentimental and possessive about children, it could be seen as a courtesy to the woman not to burden her with a child which might make her less marriageable next time round.[6] In Pictish Scotland, as I have already mentioned, women might have more than one 'husband' and lineage was traced through the mother's line, so that your status depended on who your mother was, not your father.

# FOSTERING

Fostering was common practice among the Celts, as indeed it was among the Anglo-Saxons and the Scandinavians too. In Ireland, fostering could be either for affection or for payment, and it was more expensive to have a girl fostered than a boy, because girls were viewed as more trouble and less help. The bonds between foster children and their foster parents and siblings were considered to be even closer than blood-bonds, and were sacred in fact. So we can presume that sending children to be fostered was a way of making alliances and showing trust, given that it was taboo for foster brothers to kill each other – although this did sometimes happen (see, for example, Cuchulain and Ferdia in the *Tain*). Perhaps it was also a way of arranging the right kind of education for your children. If they were clever, you might send them to be fostered in a druid household; if physically well endowed, in a warrior's family. It shows that the Celts must have had a far less sentimental and possessive view of children than we do.[5]

# CONCEPTION AND CONTRACEPTION

We know from the east Yorkshire finds that child-bearing depleted women's strength, making them vulnerable to illness and premature death, so we can guess that the Celts may well have devised means of limiting conception, if not for the woman's sake then to avoid having another mouth to feed in times of shortage. Given that the Celts and the people who came before them in Europe were capable of complex astronomical predictions and charting the cyclical passage of time (the famous Coligny Calendar found in Gaul is hard evidence of this), it would not be surprising that some of the more observant women would have noted at which times of the monthly cycle they were more likely to get pregnant. If they could avoid having sex around the mid-cycle point when they were ovulating, a time which is marked by changes in the vaginal mucus, they would not conceive.

*The White Horse of Uffington, first century BC.*
(Craig Chapman)

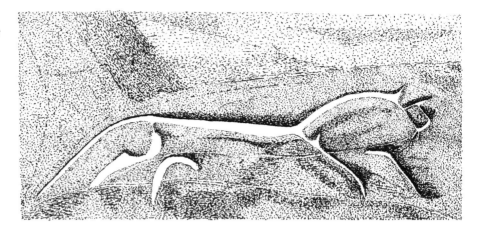

It is also likely that women living together in a close community would all menstruate at the same time, so that there could have been periods when it was either taboo to have intercourse or encouraged, and the instructions for those times could vary depending on whether the tribe needed more members or not. In addition to knowledge of this form of 'rhythm method', there may have been other means known of preventing conception, be it the use of varieties of moss to stop sperm getting past the cervix or herbs to suppress ovulation.

It could be argued that this is all speculation, but with the great barrier of the Christian revolution, which so alienated women from their bodies, standing between us and the pagan Celts, it is important not to presume that they were ignorant in the same ways that we tend to be. There is also another great barrier in the shape of the industrial revolution which uprooted people from the rural lives in which they may well have had access to ancient forms of body knowledge and thrust them into the inferno of urban factories, where they soon forgot these things. In the tale of Rhiannon from the Welsh story *Pwyll, Prince of Dyfed* in *The Mabinogion*, recorded in the thirteenth century from much older oral versions, we find traces of a lost tradition of female knowledge and wisdom.[12] Queen Rhiannon, with associations to horses and foals, seems to be a humanized form of the great goddess Epona, symbolized as a white horse, who was popular in Romano-Celtic times. As the goddess gradually loses her power, we find this event recorded in a variety of ways in the tales like the one opposite.

In this marvellous and curious story scholars believe we have several different strands of myth woven together by a master storyteller into a new and satisfying whole. In other words, we are dealing with a sophisticated product of the thirteenth century, not a vivid, raw tale which lights up the Dark and Iron Ages the way some of the Irish material does. Nevertheless, in the figure of Rhiannon we have a heroine whose power, authority and being in the world are a lot more than fairytale cliché and can tell us a great deal about the nature of women in Celtic Wales. Although the Romans did colonize Wales, their rule did not 'take' there as it had in England, and the Anglo-Saxons also failed to make an impact, so Celtic culture in Wales retained an integrity that had been lost in most of the rest of the British mainland except for Cornwall and parts of Scotland.

## *Rhiannon, Queen of the Otherworld*

THE WHITE horse slipped through the trees smoothly and sound-lessly. Pwyll blinked and rubbed his eyes. Was it a real or a dream horse? Had he fallen asleep while waiting on the Mound of Arbeth, or was this the true vision he had been longing for? He knew that anyone who came here would either receive blows or witness a wonder, depending on the will of the Otherworld. He had hoped that he, Pwyll, Prince of Dyfed, would be honoured with a wonder, since he had spent some time in that hidden, inner realm, and knew its ways.

Now he saw that a woman was riding on the horse, richly clad in a shining gold garment. Quickly he shouted to one of his men to run and catch up with her, to find out who she was. A lad did so, but try as he might he could not gain on the horsewoman at all. He rushed off to fetch his horse and tried to pursue her on horseback, but he could not get close to her that way either and eventually she faded away between the slim trunks of the silver birches.

Pwyll was fascinated by the apparition, so next day he and his men returned to the mound, this time equipped with the fastest horses, and waited for the woman to appear. When she did Pwyll sent his best men after her, but they reported the same phenomenon: they could not get close to her at all because the distance between them always stayed the same, no matter whether they ambled along or pushed their horses to the limit.

On the third day when the woman on the horse passed close by, Pwyll decided to pursue her in person, so he jumped on to his horse and set off after her. When he was within hailing distance he shouted, 'Lady, for the sake of the man you love, stop a moment!'

'Gladly I will,' she replied, 'and your horse would be glad too, if you'd thought of asking me that earlier.'

'Tell me where you come from and where you are going,' Pwyll asked breathlessly.

'I'm going about my own business,' she answered with a smile.

'What is that business?' he pressed her.

'To tell the truth, my main business was to find a way of meeting you,' she said, throwing back her veil. She had a lovely face, but what struck him most was the candour in her grey eyes and the sparkling intelligence

that animated her features. 'Here is a rare woman,' he thought, 'a woman who is in touch with the mysteries.' Pwyll was dazzled.

'I'm very happy to hear that. Will you now tell me who you are?'

'I am Rhiannon, daughter of Hefeydd the Old, who is about to hand me over in marriage to a man I do not love. I don't love him because I love you, and I came to find you, hoping that you might be able to save me from this wretched liaison.'

'Lady,' said Pwyll, 'of all the women in the world you are the only one that I could wish to marry.'

Then the two of them made a pact that in a year's time Pwyll would come to Rhiannon's father's court for a marriage feast.

In a year's time he did just that, bringing with him 100 riders, and found Hefeydd and his retinue waiting to welcome him warmly. The tables were groaning with good food; he was seated to one side of Hefeydd and Rhiannon to the other. After the meal, when the singing was beginning, a tall, fine-looking youth with auburn hair and royal mien entered the hall. Pwyll greeted him cordially and asked him to sit down and join in the feast.

'I will not,' said the young man, 'because I am a suitor not a guest and I have come to ask you for something.'

'What is it?' asked Pwyll jovially. 'Rest assured that whatever it is you shall have it, if it is in my power to give.'

'Oh, no!' Rhiannon hissed across the table. 'You should not have made such a rash promise!'

'But it's too late,' said the youth. 'He has made the promise in the presence of nobles.'

'Friend, what is your request?' asked Pwyll.

'It's simply this: the lady I love you are to sleep with tonight. I have come to ask for her and for this feast and all the preparations for the wedding.'

Pwyll was struck dumb.

'Stay dumb as long as you want,' said Rhiannon angrily. 'I have never seen anyone act more stupidly than you have just now.'

'But, lady,' said Pwyll in anguish, 'I didn't know who he was.'

'He is the man they would have given me to against my will, Gwawl, son of Clud, and now, because you have given your word, you will have to hand me over to him, for fear of dishonour.'

'Lady, I could never ever bring myself to do that!'

All eyes at the court were on Rhiannon as she stood behind Pwyll's seat, talking to him in a low and agitated voice. Then she paused and brought herself under control, smiling for the benefit of the audience, speaking now in a calm, even voice.

'Listen carefully. You have no choice now but to give me to him. Don't worry, I shall arrange that he shall never have me. He's asked for the feast

*Rhiannon, Queen of the Otherworld, on her magical white horse.*

and all the wedding preparations too. Tell him they are not yours to give. He must return in a year's time when a feast will be prepared especially for him. Everything else I will explain later.'

Gwawl was getting restless. Pwyll spoke to him as Rhiannon had instructed and he nodded and departed well satisfied. Then Rhiannon told Pwyll the details of her plan and the part he must play in it, and arranged to meet him at the feast in one year's time.

The next year Gwawl son of Clud arrived for his marriage feast and was warmly welcomed in Hefeydd's court. Pwyll arrived too, and waited outside the hall dressed in shabby beggar's garments and big rag boots until he knew the guests had finished eating and were ready to carouse. Then he made his entrance, and humbly asked Gwawl to fulfil one request.

'I will,' said Gwawl warily, 'as long as it is a reasonable one.'

'It's just to fill this little bag with food.'

'That seems fair enough. Bring this man food,' Gwawl commanded. But as soon as food was put into the bag it was swallowed up so that the bag still seemed half empty.

'Will your bag ever be full?' asked Gwawl.

'Only when a man of great power and many possessions tramples down the food in it and says enough is enough!'

Taking the hint, Gwawl leapt up and jumped into the bag, but as soon as his feet had touched it Pwyll bounded to his side and pulled it up around him, tying the two tapes at its neck so that Gwawl was trapped in the bag. Then Pwyll's men, who had been hidden, erupted into the hall and took Gwawl's men prisoner. They each of them came up and had a kick at the bag, pretending that it had a badger in it. (This is how the game of 'Badger in the Bag' was invented.)

After a few minutes of this tomfoolery, Rhiannon intervened and advised Pwyll to be merciful and let Gwawl out of the bag as long as he promised to go away and not seek revenge, which the bruised and battered man did. Then Pwyll went to sit at his rightful place at the table and the feast continued. That night he and Rhiannon slept together and in the morning set off for Pwyll's kingdom of Dyfed.

At first the citizens of Dyfed welcomed Rhiannon warmly, but in the third year of her marriage to their king still no child had been produced and they began to try to persuade Pwyll to put her aside and choose another more fecund wife. But Pwyll asked for a little more time and indeed, within a year, Rhiannon was pregnant and had given birth to a healthy son.

However the morning after his birth, while Rhiannon was sleeping, her women entered the bedchamber to find that the baby had disappeared. Terrified that they would be punished for this mysterious disaster, they killed a couple of puppies and smeared the blood on to their mistress's face and clothes, to make it look as if she had murdered her own child.

When Rhiannon awoke, her women told her that she had gone berserk in the night, that they had struggled with her but to no avail, that she had torn her new-born son limb from limb and feasted on the remains. Rhiannon protested that this was not true and promised them that they would not be punished if they told the truth about what had happened, but nothing would make them retract their lies. Then Pwyll was informed of the tragedy and his chief advisers rushed to tell him he must certainly put his wife away now, after this terrible crime. But Pwyll said, 'You wanted me to discard my wife because she had no children. I know she has a child now, and I will not put her away, but if she has done wrong, let her do penance.'

Rhiannon summoned her teachers and wise men and women and asked for their counsel. With their help she decided to accept a penance rather than get involved in a wrangle with her women. The penance was that for seven years she must sit by the horse-block at the gate to the city and tell the whole story of her child's disappearance to everyone who came in and then offer to carry them on her back wherever they needed to go. In other words she was to turn herself into a beast of burden.

Meanwhile, an extraordinary thing had happened at the house of one of the finest men in the country. Every year Teyrnon and his wife, who were childless, had their best foal snatched by a clawed monster as soon as it was born. This year Teyrnon decided this must stop, so he lay in wait for the monster at night and hacked its gigantic claw off with his sword as it poked through the window of the house. When he dashed outside to pursue the beast, he found a beautiful baby boy lying on the ground wrapped in rich brocade. Because his wife had always longed for a child, Teyrnon gave the boy to her and together they brought him up. He was no ordinary child, but able to walk on his own well before he was one, and as big as a child of six when he was only two. And before he was even four he was bargaining with the grooms to let him take his beloved horses to water, so his foster parents gave him the young horse who had been saved from the monster on the same night that he had come into their lives.

But by now Teyrnon, a very honourable man, could no longer conceal from himself the fact that his foster son looked remarkably like Pwyll, the king, and so one day he and his foster son and his retinue made their way to Arberth. They were met by Rhiannon at the gate.

'Chieftain,' she said, 'go no further. I will carry each one of you to the court on my back. This is my penance for killing my own son with my bare hands.'

'Lady,' said Teyrnon gently, 'I do not think that anyone in this party will consent to be carried on your back.'

'I certainly won't,' said Teyrnon's foster son fiercely.

Rhiannon was puzzled, but Teyrnon begged her to wait, and together they walked up to the court to see Pwyll. As soon as the boy was seen with his rightful mother and father there could be no doubt in anyone's mind that he belonged to them.

'See, Lady,' said Teyrnon, 'those who told lies against you are proved wrong. This boy is certainly your son.'

'If this is true,' said Rhiannon, 'then I am freed at last from my anguish and my care.'

And so it was that Rhiannon named her son 'Pryderi' which means 'care' or 'thought'. He grew up to be a much-loved ruler in Dyfed, and Rhiannon lived on to have other strange and wonderful adventures in both this world and the other.

The story presents Rhiannon as intelligent, assertive, wise and ingenious. She makes a decisive play for the man she wants, rejecting the patriarchal order represented by her father. When her beloved is stupid, her knowledge of human nature and her magical skills save the day. But as a woman of the Otherworld, she has much to lose in marriage with a man of the ordinary world because she will be forced to live by its rules rather than her own. She delays conception of her first child, perhaps by knowledge of herbs or an understanding of body cycles, but must produce an heir to please Pwyll's subjects. When her baby is snatched, her women try to destroy her, but instead of fighting them or tying to destroy them, she takes on a penance, after consulting her teachers and wise men.

This is a woman who is being instructed in some kind of inner wisdom, taught to understand that things are often not what they seem, that there is another order beyond the everyday which only the initiated may know about. Indeed, Pwyll's first meeting with her, in which he keeps vigil on a magical mound, has resonances of an initiation rite: the young man is not allowed to enter the female realm of the Otherworld until he learns how to approach it in the right way.

In the elements of the story which concern the baby snatched by a monster, we may have traces of memory of times when wolves or other marauding beasts sometimes took and killed small children, or it may be a way of dealing with the custom of exposing sickly, disabled or unwanted children who would be left out in the wild to die, unless rescued by someone who took pity on them. The bones of babies have been found buried in the foundations of Celtic forts, suggesting that they may have been sacrificed to ensure the prosperity of the settlements. These themes could not be explicit in a story written down in the relatively civilized thirteenth century, but they are still present in a compressed and distorted form, just as symbols in dreams contain all sorts of ideas repressed by consciousness which can be unpacked again via careful interpretation.

Rhiannon herself certainly seems to represent a highly developed type of woman. The original Rhiannon was a horse goddess, or the priestess of this goddess, who would perform rites associated with her mysteries. Perhaps one of her jobs was to guard the boundaries between the worlds, or lead people from one world to another. In a different tale in *The Mabinogion* there is a reference to 'the birds of Rhiannon', whose song 'wakes the dead and lulls the living to sleep'. These birds also sing in another tale at the point when a band of weary warriors begins a journey towards the Otherworld. Rhiannon's birds seem to be both the messengers of that world and its guardians.

At the very least the story of Rhiannon tells of a culture where it is possible for a woman to be regarded as an equal to her husband, and where a woman's wit and wisdom are sometimes considered superior to a man's. Rhiannon still retains some of the power and glamour of the Goddess, and Pwyll, a man of wisdom himself, is rightly in awe of that. In addition the story can profitably be analysed at a psychological level, as an account of the growing up and maturation of a woman. I am sure many women with small children can easily see themselves as sentenced to seven years as a 'beast of burden'!

# 4 THE GOLDEN AGE OF THE MOTHER GODDESS

## *DID IT EVER EXIST?*

In the early 1980s I produced a TV comedy programme called *Revolting Women* and part of it was a weekly serial, *Bogwomen*, which concerned an ancient matriarchal tribe living in the bogs outside Personchester, worshipping the Goddess and having as little as possible to do with men. *Bogwomen* was attempting to satirize the notion beloved by many feminists that there had once been a peaceful matriarchal age, before men spoilt everything by being aggressive and rough. Even though we poked fun at these fantasies, we half believed them ourselves, as many people still do, happily ignoring the fact that the academic community of anthropologists and archaeologists have come down against the likelihood of such a society ever existing.

Instead, scholars now believe that there may well have been goddess-worshipping cultures, probably hunter-gatherers, in which the relations between men and women, in particular the power balance between them, *may* have been very different from what it became in later patriarchal societies. But, they point out, the fact that a goddess was venerated does not necessarily mean that individual women had power or status, or were protected from the depredations of male – or female – violence. For instance, it could be that the earth goddess would require the sacrifice of young virgins in order to ensure the fertility of the land. Bani Shorter has suggested that this kind of sacrifice may be at the root of the story of Persephone, who is kidnapped by Hades and taken down into the land of the dead; maybe thc original Persephone was actually killed.[13] There are legends in British folklore which hint at similar sacrifices.

However, the position of women in a goddess-based culture is not going to be similar to their position within today's western patriarchal Christian culture. The strength and power of the female, her community with the female god-form, would have to be acknowledged. The male gods, especially in their son or consort form, like Adonis or Osiris, will tend to be seen as either servants or at best partners of the Goddess. Only when they become powerful 'our-fathers' does female power begin to be seriously diminished.

# THE MOTHER GODDESS – THE EVIDENCE

What evidence is there to suggest that the Celtic societies, or rather the European peoples who pre-dated them, were once matri-centred or goddess-worshipping? The most intriguing and suggestive evidence comes from the Irish *Lebor Gabala*, the *Book of Invasions*, which purports to give a history of the peoples who inhabited Ireland from the beginning of time. It was written down first in the eighth century AD, although we have only later versions now. It claims that the first settlers in Ireland were led by a woman called Cessair, who was accompanied by a predominantly female band of supporters. Her consort, Fintan, is a shape-shifter who spends time as a salmon, an eagle and a hawk. This sounds like a matri-centred shamanistic culture, or at least a society where male and female power was fairly equally balanced, as it may have been among hunter-gatherer peoples.

One of the later waves of invaders, the Fomoire, also seems to represent the feminine, because each of their ships' companies comprises 50 men and 150 women. Chichol's monstrous mother, Lot, a bloated creature with her lips in her breast and four eyes in her back, is said to equal all her troops in strength. Lot sounds very much like a caricature of the Great Goddess created by men who fear her but acknowledge her power.

In addition the famous Tuatha De Danann – the Children of Dana (or Don) – are actually called after their mother, the trans-European Mother Goddess, Dana, who gave her name to rivers as far apart as the Don in Yorkshire, the Danube in Germany and perhaps even the Dnieper and Dniester in Eastern Europe. They are the most skilful and magical of the various waves of invaders, and are said to have brought the four great talismans, or magical instruments, of Ireland to her shores: the stone called the Great Fal, which shrieked when a future king sat on it (which you can still see at Tara), the Spear of Lug, the Sword of Nuada and the Cauldron of the Dagda. It is interesting to note that two of these are female symbols, in terms of shape and quality – the stone and the cauldron – and two male – the spear and the sword. When the Tuatha are defeated by the Fomoire, they take refuge in the fairy hills called the mounds of the *sidhe* (pronounced 'shee'). As I have already pointed out, the supernatural world has an essentially feminine quality in the Irish tradition: women are far more prominent than men in the medieval accounts of magical mound-dwellings and islands of immortality. It is from the Tuatha De Danann that the goddess Brigit seems to originate; even to the present day in her form as St Brigit she is a powerful feminine spiritual force (see Chapter 5).

All this does seem to suggest that in Ireland at least the Goddess was once the pre-eminent power. It has also been noted that all the great ancient centres of power are named after goddesses: Tara after the goddess Tea (according to one story), Tailtiu after Tailtiu, Emain Macha after Macha. Many rivers and settlements are also named for goddesses or sorceresses.

53

Left: *The Paps of Anu –
the Great Mother
embedded in the
landscape.*
(Paddy Dillon)

The Great Mother has embedded herself unforgettably into the land. But what happened to her power in later times?

It is known that the rulers of Ireland were men, kings whose queens were more or less prominent but certainly did not rule equally with their mates. Nevertheless, when Giraldus Cambrensis visited Ireland in the late twelfth century, he claimed to have witnessed a bizarre scene at the inauguration of the high king. A white mare was led in and the king either actually copulated or enacted copulation with her, after which she was killed and boiled up in a cauldron. The king then bathed in the broth and ate of the flesh of the beast.

It sounds barbarous to us, and equally so to Giraldus, no doubt, but we should not let that blind us to the fact that the mare here is actually standing in for the goddess of sovereignty, the sacred embodiment of the land. In many of the mythological tales she appears in person, often as an ugly old hag who, when kissed by the hero/king, turns into a beautiful woman.

## The Morrigan Meets the Dagda

**b**EFORE the second battle of Moytura the great god Dagda of the Tuatha De Danann met up with the goddess Morrigan as she was washing in the river Unshin with one foot planted on either side of the water. He copulated with her in that position and afterwards she told him where the enemy host of the Fomoire would land, and promised that she would break the spirit of the enemy king by draining away his valour and 'the blood from his heart'. Later she and her two equally fearsome sisters, Badb and Macha, would bring hailstones and fierce showers down upon the enemy and fling javelins and flails against them.[10]

Opposite: *The trans-
European Mother
Goddess, Dana.*

## *Niall of the Nine Hostages and the Goddess*

**n**IALL was the son of King Eochu by his concubine, but the king had four other sons by his wife, Mongfhind, so there was some argument about which of them should inherit the kingship. One day the five brothers were hunting in the forest when they came upon a hideously ugly old woman at a well. She refused to give them water unless they were prepared to kiss her cheek. They all refused except Niall, who embraced her and lay down with her on the grass. Immediately she turned into a beautiful girl and told Niall he should give water to his brothers only on the condition that they let him place his weapons higher than theirs in Tara. When Niall told his father about this, his brothers accepted his primacy and it was declared that he and his descendants would have dominion over Ireland.[10]

The message of these tales and others like them is that the king may not reign unless he unites with the Goddess of the Land. She is the guardian of the power he needs in order to rule and she will bestow this power on him only if he behaves in a fitting manner towards her. There must be traces here of very ancient rites which accompanied the making of a king. Possibly the king did copulate with a priestess who represented the Goddess of the Land.

*Sheela-na-gig from Ballyparty Castle, Ireland; the goddess as sexually voracious hag.* (Craig Chapman)

Certainly we know that he had to drink the 'ale of Cuala' given to him from her hand. This sacred fluid, like the water which the woman gives Niall, symbolizes the power which the Goddess of the Land transfers to the rightful king, the same liquid referred to in the name 'Maeve', which means 'intoxicating one'. We could even speculate that originally these fluids might have been the juices produced in the vagina of a sexually aroused woman or even her menstrual blood. Certainly the intoxication referred to could be that of sexual ecstasy, which, like battle ecstasy, gives a taste of the glory of the divine world.[14]

## Queen Maeve of Connacht

Cuchulain is supposed to be the hero of the *Tain Bo Cuailnge*, but the character who really jumps out from the narrative is his enemy, the wicked Queen Maeve. The whole tale is too long to tell in this book, and a large part of it has nothing to do with women, being the record of Cuchulain's various victories over Maeve's champions, but it is basically the story of the battle between Ulster and Connacht which starts when Maeve decides she wants the magnificent brown bull of Cooley for herself, so as to be one up on her husband, Ailill, who is now the owner of Finnbennach, a marvellous white bull which used to belong to her but went over to her husband because he didn't like being led by a woman.

Queen Maeve in the *Tain* is both an embodiment of sovereignty and a sexually voracious matriarch who moves through a series of king-lovers, giving each of them in turn the right to rule. Another Maeve, Maeve of Lethberg, was the wife of nine of the kings of Ireland in succession: they could not be king unless they were married to her. In the *Tain* you can clearly sense the presence of a spirit of resentment against this female power, and the storyteller dramatizes this by making Maeve ruthless, cruel and devious, as well as sexually voracious, while the hero she is up against, Cuchulain, is honourable and selfless. The story is full of little needling asides against women and the clearest moral of the story is that women make bad rulers. Fergus actually says at the end, after the men of Connacht have been defeated, 'We followed the rump of a misguiding woman. It is the usual thing for a herd led by a mare to be strayed and destroyed.'

Although this funny and exciting story is a clever piece of anti-woman propaganda, it would be wrong to take too much exception to it, because Maeve is an irresistible comic creation, magnificent in her awfulness. All the men, except Cuchulain (who has the kind of sombre machine-like heroism which Arnold Schwarzenegger has so well perfected), pale beside her. In stories wickedness is usually more interesting than goodness, and Maeve's enjoyable badness is really a backhanded acknowledgement of her power. Listen to Thomas Kinsella's masterly translation of Maeve and Ailill's pillow talk, the conversation which starts the war.

## The Pillow Talk

ONCE when the royal bed was laid out for Ailill and Maeve in Cruachan fort in Connacht, they had this talk on the pillows. 'It is true what they say, love,' Ailill said. 'It is well for the wife of a wealthy man.'

'True enough,' the woman said. 'What put that in your mind?'

'It struck me,' Ailill said, 'how much better off you are today than the day I married you.'

'I was well enough off without you,' Maeve said.

'Then your wealth was something I didn't know or hear much about,' Ailill said. 'Except for your woman's things, and the neighbouring enemies making off with loot and plunder.'

'Not at all,' Maeve said, 'but with the high king of Ireland for my father . . . I had 1,500 soldiers in my royal pay, all exiles' sons, and the same number of free-born native men, and for every paid soldier I had ten more men, and nine more, and eight, and seven, and six, and five, and four, and three, and two, and one. And that was only our ordinary household.

'My father gave me the whole province of Ireland, this province ruled from Cruachan, which is why I am called "Maeve of Cruachan". And they came from Finn the king of Leinster, Rus Ruad's son, to woo me, and from Coirpre Niafer the king of Temair, another of Rus Ruad's sons. They came from Conchobar, king of Ulster, son of Fachtna, and they came from Eochaid Bec, and I wouldn't go. For I asked a harder wedding gift than any woman ever asked before from a man in Ireland – the absence of meanness and jealousy and fear.

'If I married a mean man our union would be wrong, because I'm so full of grace and giving. It would be an insult if I were more generous than my husband, but not if the two of us were equal in this. If my husband was a timid man our union would be just as wrong because I thrive, myself, on all kinds of trouble. It is an insult for a wife to be more spirited than her husband, but not if the two are equally spirited. If I married a jealous man that would be wrong too; I never had one man without another waiting in his shadow. So I got the kind of man I wanted: Rus Ruad's other son – yourself, Ailill, from Leinster. You aren't greedy or jealous or sluggish. When you were promised, I brought you the best wedding gift a bride can bring: apparel enough for a dozen men, a chariot worth thrice seven bondmaids, the width of your face of red gold and the weight of your left arm of light gold. So, if anyone causes you shame or upset or trouble, the right to compensation is mine,' Maeve said, 'for you're a kept man.'

'By no means,' Ailill said, 'but with two kings for my brothers, Coirpre in Temair and Finn over Leinster. I let them rule because they were older,

*Maeve and Ailill.*

not because they are better than I in grace of giving. I never heard, in all Ireland, of a province run by a woman except this one, which is why I came and took the kingship here, in succession to my mother, Mata Muiresc, Magach's daughter. Who better for my queen than you, a daughter of the high king of Ireland?'

'It still remains,' Maeve said, 'that my fortune is greater than yours.'

'You amaze me,' Ailill said. 'No one has more property or jewels or precious things than I have, and I know it.'

The fact that the Irish and Welsh vernacular literature, written down in the Middle Ages, is full of strong, characterful, interesting women is perhaps the most decisive evidence of all that these were once matri-centred cultures. The Christian monks who wrote the stories down did not on the whole diminish the women in them or turn them into saintly goody-goodies, probably because their mothers, like Adamnan's adamant mother, Ronnat, were a force to be reckoned with, as in my experience Scottish and Irish mothers and grandmothers tend to be! This view of women might be reinforced by the fact that most monks would come from the noble classes, where women could combine the hauteur of social status with a natural sense of self-worth. It is undeniable, on the other hand, that the myths and tales are also full of conflicts between male and female, where it would seem as if the patriarchal warriors are struggling to wrest power away from the matriarchal figures. This is a theme vividly present in the story of Arianrhod from the tale *Math Son of Mathonwy* in *The Mabinogion*.[12]

## Arianrhod, the Virgin Mother

GILFAETHWY was suffering terribly from the pangs of unrequited love. He was infatuated to the point that he was losing weight and growing pale, becoming unrecognizable to his friends. The problem was that the object of his desires was Goewin, the most beautiful girl of her time, and footholder to the Lord Math, Gilfaethwy's uncle. She had been given the job because she was a virgin. Math was a famous sage and magician, but he was under a strange spell: unless he was caught up in a war, he had to sit with his feet resting in the fold of a virgin's lap. If his feet touched the ground he would die.

One day Gilfaethwy's brother, Gwydion, guessing what the matter with him was, proposed a solution: he would create trouble between the different principalities of Wales, so that in the disarray his brother could get access to Goewin and satisfy the desire which was making him ill.

And so it was that he mounted an elaborate trick on Pryderi, the ruler of the south of Wales, persuading him by magic and enchantment to part with a wonderful new variety of pig which he had brought to Wales. Gwydion's magic was to create the semblance of some marvellous horses and dogs so that Pryderi would swap his pigs for them. But Gwydion knew the magic would not last long, so he and his brother set forth with all speed back to their uncle's court before their ruse could be found out.

They told Math that the pigs were safe in a newly built sty, but that Pryderi and his forces were on their heels, so Math mustered his army and set out to meet the enemy. That night the two brothers sneaked back to Math's castle and dragged Goewin away from the girls who attended her. Then Gilfaethwy forced Goewin into his uncle's bed with him, and made love to her, much against her will.

The next day the brothers joined battle with their uncle against Pryderi's forces. There was terrible slaughter until Pryderi suggested that the matter should be settled by single combat between himself and Gwydion, who was after all the cause of the trouble. Gwydion agreed and fought with Pryderi. It was not a fair fight because Gwydion had not only strength and courage on his side but also his magical arts. Unsurprisingly he killed the noble Pryderi and won the day.

The score thus bitterly settled, Math's party released the hostages they held and Pryderi's men marched sadly south. Math was sad too because he had great respect for Pryderi. He returned to his court and went to his bedchamber, to put his feet on Goewin's lap.

Goewin forestalled him.

'No, sir,' she said, 'you need a virgin for this job and I am a woman now.'

'How is that?' asked Math, shocked.

'While you were away your two nephews came, and I was taken by Gilfaethwy and although I shouted and screamed for help, it was no use. He took me into your bed and slept with me. I was raped and you have been dishonoured.'

Math laid his hand on the girl's head.

'Don't worry,' he said quietly. 'First I shall arrange compensation for you, and then for myself: I will marry you and give authority over my realm into your hands.'

Meanwhile Gwydion and Gilfaethwy had been making themselves scarce, but eventually an order went out that no one was to give them food or drink, so that they were forced to return to their uncle's court.

'So you have come back to make amends, have you?' he asked them coldly.

'Lord,' they replied, 'we are at your service.'

'If you had been at my service, I wouldn't have lost all those good men and their arms. I would not have been dishonoured. Neither would Pryderi

61

have died. However, since you have come to me, I will give you a punishment.'

He took his magic wand and struck Gilfaethwy with it so that he was transformed into a hind. At this Gwydion tried to run away but Math quickly struck him with the same wand, so that he became a stag.

'Now,' he said, 'you will go off and live in the wild as these animals, partaking in their nature. You will copulate with each other and have offspring. Come again in a year.'

In a year's time they came, bringing along with them a young fawn. Math turned the one who was a stag into a sow and the one who was a hind into a wild boar. And the fawn he turned into a young boy and sent him off to be fostered.

The next year, the two brothers returned in their animal forms again, this time with a sturdy young boar at their side. Math turned them into two wolves this time, one of either sex, and sent them off to live in the wild together for another year.

A year later, hearing barking outside his chamber, Math looked out to see the two wolves with a lively cub. He promised to turn the cub into a boy and have him fostered along with the other two of his nephews' offspring. Then he struck Gwydion and Gilfaethwy with his wand and turned them back into themselves.

*Gilfaethwy and Gwydion were transformed into wolves to teach them a lesson.*
(Bruce Tanner)

'You have been punished enough,' he said, 'and suffered the shame of each having to bear young by the other. Now go off and have a bath and make yourselves human again.'

When they came back, Math said, 'Boys, your ordeals are over. Let us put our differences behind us and be friends again. Give me your advice. I need a new footholder. Whom shall I choose?'

'That's easy,' replied Gwydion. 'Our sister Arianrhod is exactly what you need.'

Arianrhod was brought to the king.

'Are you a virgin?' asked Math.

'In so far as I know,' she replied, her cheeks reddening with anger.

'Well, let's make sure. I am going to take this wand, bend it and ask you to step over it. If you are not a virgin, we will soon know!'

Unwillingly Arianrhod stepped over the wand. As she did so a yellow-haired boy baby tumbled out of her with a loud, lusty wail. She made a dash for the door and something else fell from under her skirts. Whatever it was, Gwydion snatched it up and wrapped it in silk before anyone could get a good look at it. Later he hid it in the chest at the foot of his bed.

Math chuckled.

'So she's a virgin, is she? Well, at least I will have this bouncing boy baptized. I shall call him Dylan.'

After the boy was baptized he made straight for the sea, where he seemed to belong, because he could swim like a fish. It was said that no wave ever broke beneath him.

Meanwhile, Gwydion was waked from his sleep one morning by the wailing of a child, and when he opened his chest he saw a baby boy pushing aside the sheets tucked around him with his little fat arms. Gwydion was thrilled to have his own child and took him straight into town and arranged a wet nurse.

The boy grew up quickly and loved Gwydion more than anyone, but Gwydion knew deep down that Arianrhod was the child's mother, so one day he took the boy to her castle. Arianrhod's castle stood on cliffs at the edge of the sea. It was round in shape and translucent. Sometimes it would be seen to revolve slowly, catching and reflecting the light on its crystalline facets as it turned. Arianrhod greeted her brother warily.

'Who is the boy with you?' she asked.

'Your son, of course. Who else?'

'How could you do this to me? You shamed me then, and now you come to rub salt in my wound.'

'What is your shame compared to mine if I'd refused to rear the boy?'

'What's his name?'

'He does not have one yet.'

'In that case I swear that he shall never have one unless he gets it from me.'

'And I swear that he shall have one, however much it hurts you. You are a wicked woman. You're doing this because you lost your virginity when you conceived this child, and now you will never again be able to call yourself virgin!'

With that he stormed out with the boy and went away to plot how with his magic he could trick Arianrhod into naming her son.

The next day the two of them went to the seashore and Gwydion made a ship by magic. Out of seaweed he made leather and coloured it beautifully. They sailed to Arianrhod's castle and tied up in the harbour next to it in a position in which they could be seen from the ramparts. But first of all Gwydion put an enchantment on himself and the boy so that they looked completely unlike themselves.

Soon Arianrhod spotted them from her chamber above the harbour and sent messengers to see what they were doing. When she was told that they were shoemakers, she had her feet measured and asked her servants to get the men to make her some shoes. But craftily Gwydion made sure the first pair he made, although exquisitely decorated with gold, were just a little too big, so that Arianrhod had to send them back. The next pair he made just a little too small, so that those had to be returned as well. Then Gwydion told the servants to ask the lady to come down herself to be measured and she agreed to do it.

While she stood chatting with Gwydion as he finished off the shoes, the boy spotted a wren perching on the edge of the boat and, taking up his little sling, aimed a shot which caught the bird on its leg. Arianrhod laughed admiringly.

'Surely the fair child has a very deft hand,' she said.

'Indeed he has,' said Gwydion triumphantly, 'and now you have named him in spite of yourself. From now on he will be called Lleu Llaw Gyffes, the fair deft-handed one.'

As he spoke, the magic shoes he was making vanished from his hands and Arianrhod realized she had been tricked.

'You know, you will not do yourself any good in the long run by being bad to me.'

'I haven't been bad to you yet,' said Gwydion as he dissolved the spell which disguised the pair of them.

'In that case,' countered Arianrhod, 'I swear a new destiny on the boy – that he shall never bear arms until I myself give them to him.'

'You can be as wicked as you like, but the boy will have arms, I swear it.'

Gwydion's second trick was even cleverer: he and Lleu disguised themselves once more and came to Arianrhod's court claiming to be bards. She let them in and that night after dinner Gwydion told some wonderful stories. You will not be surprised to hear that he was a brilliant teller of tales! The next morning at dawn he summoned up his magic and created a great uproar outside the gates of the castle, as if an army were preparing to attack. In her agitation Arianrhod turned to the two young men, who asked her to provide them with arms so that they could defend the castle.

She and her ladies rushed off to bring swords and shields from the store and when they returned Gwydion told her to arm the boy while he armed himself. But when they were both completely kitted out he turned to Lleu and told him to take all his equipment off again because he no longer needed it.

'But why?' asked Arianrhod. 'Surely the fleet is mustering outside.'

'The only mustering that's going on,' said Gwydion delightedly, 'is our mustering against the destiny you tried to impose on your son. Now he is armed in spite of your spite.'

'A vile trick from a vile man,' hissed Arianrhod, 'but I vow that this boy will never have a wife who belongs to the human race.'

To Gwydion this seemed the last straw, a particularly vindictive stroke of vengefulness, so he took Lleu, now a young man, to the court of Math and complained bitterly to the king about Arianrhod's actions.

'Well,' mused Math, 'a handsome young man such as he must have a wife, so we will just have to make him one, out of flowers.'

They took the flowers of the oak and of the broom and of the meadowsweet, and conjured up a young woman of extraordinary, super-human beauty, and named her Blodeuedd, which means 'flowers'. And after the wedding feast and the blissful first night Math bestowed one of his best pieces of land on the young man, so that he was well set up for life.

One day when Lleu had left his home to visit Math and Blodeuedd was on her own, she heard the sound of a horn and found out from her servants that Gronw Bebyr, Lord of Penllyn, was hunting nearby. Courtesy demanded that she invite him in, and after he had changed his clothes they sat down to talk. But as soon as Blodeuedd looked at Gronw she was filled with love for him, and he felt the same towards her.

He stayed the night, and the next night, and as he left in the morning he and Blodeuedd plotted to find a way to kill her husband. And while she was in bed with Lleu that night Blodeuedd managed to tease out of him the strange taboos surrounding his death: he could only be killed by a spear made over the course of a year while the people were at mass; he could not be killed either within a house or outside one, on horseback or on foot. Then while Lleu was relaxed and half asleep Blodeuedd got him to go over the peculiar circumstances which would need to be arranged if he was ever to be killed: he would need to stand with one foot on the edge of a bath placed by a river and the other on a he-goat, with a vaulted frame of thatch over him. Then he could be killed by the specially prepared spear.

Opposite: *Arianrhod, the virgin mother who guards the women's mysteries.*

'Well, thank God for that,' murmured Blodeuedd, 'that circumstance can easily be avoided!'

But in a year's time, when Gronw had prepared the magical spear, she persuaded Lleu to show her exactly how it would have to be, if he were to be killed, and they went to the riverbank and set up the bath and the thatch and the he-goat. Once Lleu was balancing in place, Gronw jumped out from where he had been hidden and threw the spear at Lleu.

The spear pierced Lleu. With a horrid scream he flew up into the air in the form of an eagle and was gone.

Gronw took over Lleu's wife and land while grief-stricken Gwydion set off to comb the country in search of his beloved nephew. Eventually he came across a wise old sow who led him to a tree where she was feeding on rotten flesh and maggots dropping down from the body of a pathetic skinny eagle who sat in the topmost branches.

Gwydion knew the eagle was Lleu. It flew down and alighted on his knee. Then he touched it with his magic wand and it became a man, a pitiful creature of skin and bone, but Lleu nevertheless.

Good doctors restored Lleu to health over a year and then he set off to do vengeance: he turned Blodeuedd into an owl, a creature which must fly by night and is spurned by the other birds, and he made Gronw return to the riverbank with him, where he killed him with a spear that pierced straight through the rock which Gronw had asked to be set between them. So was justice done.

And Arianrhod in her revolving castle watched and grieved and thought how different it all could have been, if her son had not been untimely ripped from her by his uncle, her brother.

Left: *Blodeuedd is transformed into a barn owl, which also symbolizes Arianrhod the Lady of Light.*
(Mike Read)

Math the magician cannot function as a king unless he has his two feet in the fold of a virgin's lap. What on earth is this about? The 'lap' could certainly be a euphemism for the female genitals, and the 'feet' for the male. It may be the remnant of a tradition whereby the king would copulate with a virgin priestess representing the Goddess as part of his inauguration. But, as the power of the Goddess waned, the term 'virgin' changed from meaning 'a woman who belongs to no man' to 'a woman who has not been penetrated by a man', so that the role of 'footholder' would be a way of remembering the tradition without falling into paradox: the king can't sleep with a 'virgin' because she won't remain a virgin if he does, but he can be connected to the sacred earth via her 'lap'.

At any rate the king's nephews (in a matrilineal society sister's sons would be especially beloved) play a devious trick to get Goewin on her own and rape her. This rape deprives her of her magical role as virgin footholder, so it is even more than a physical and emotional assault. When she complains to Math later of the abuse, we can sense how seriously they both regard it. Math the king behaves well towards Goewin. He represents the old order of men who respect the power of the female and wish to stay in harmony with it; as king he plans to share his authority with her, his new queen. His nephews, on the other hand, are clever, arrogant young men of the new warrior élite who wish to steal women's power, tear the veil from their mysteries and even take over the sacred female functions of conception and birth. The king deliberately chooses to punish his nephews by making them experience their animal natures and take turns to be a female animal who conceives and gives birth. This is meant to make them respect the female principle but it does not work, because their next crime is to press their sister Arianrhod into the service of the king.

Now Arianrhod was once a goddess, and although humanized in the story, she still has magical power and a magical role. She may be seen as a priestess of the old order, a 'virgin' on women's terms not men's – that is a woman who does not belong to one man, who serves the Goddess and, via her, the whole of humankind. There might be no reason for this priestess-Arianrhod to be *technically* a virgin, although she would probably sleep with men only as part of a holy rite, to initiate them into the mysteries of the Goddess. But, of course, Math's test proves that she is not a virgin in male terms: the stepping over of the wand sounds like a euphemism for examination or penetration, either one an outrageous profaning of her mysteries.

At any rate, she is forced or tricked by brutal male magic into giving birth to two sons. The first, Dylan, is made for the sea, and Moyra Caldecott suggests, I think rightly, that his father may have been Manannan mac Llyr, the sea god.[15] The second 'little something' is snatched away by Gwydion and put in a chest, embodying a fantasy that men can actually take over and control the process of reproduction from women (coming frighteningly true now in our age of 'assisted conception'). He wants to make his sister's child his own, cut out female interference in the creation of a magical child. It is also possible that Lleu *is* actually his child, conceived by incest with his sister.

So the battle between brother and sister, male and female, men's and women's mysteries begins. The tradition that a mother or her representative must name, arm and find a mate for her son may date back to times when the magical roles of the two sexes were better understood. Gwydion ruthlessly exploits his male magic to force Arianrhod to 'complete' the son she started in her womb. She resists with protective vows; what she is defending is the woman's right to own her body and what comes out of it. Gwydion cannot defeat her taboos directly; he must circumvent them craftily with clever shape-shifter's magic.

In the delightful 'three tricks' sequence each side calls the other wicked, but the truth is that the male–female polarity is out of kilter, with the man trying to invade the woman's sacred space of creation and the woman defending herself in the only way she can, by refusing to co-operate in this abomination. The third trick, of making a woman out of flowers, takes us straight into *Stepford Wives* territory. Man makes woman in his own image because he cannot bear the power and cussedness of real women, but the woman made to fulfil the male fantasies will destroy him in the end because she lacks that essential secret inner space that all real women have, in which is hidden her integrity, her being and her existence apart and separate from the male. It is interesting that Blodeuedd, the 'man's woman', is clever in the devious, tricksterish way of her creator, very much in the cold-blooded way that women who adopt male values often are.

It seems at the end of the story that the clever male magicians have won the day, but in fact the reader knows in her heart of hearts that the defiant spirit of Arianrhod (as with Deirdre and Maeve) cannot be crushed without causing terrible suffering to all: the delicate balance of power between the sexes is not to be messed with!

Arianrhod's name means 'silver circle' and she is one version of the Celtic Lady of Light. You can still visit the site of her castle. It used to stand in the bay at Tregar Antbrag, just opposite Dinas Dinlle, the Castle of Lleu, which is present as a rocky mound overlooking the sea. Particularly at dawn and dusk, if you look out westwards over the water, you will be able to see the shimmering crystal palace rise up from the waves and build itself out of flashes and glimmerings of light for a moment before vanishing again into the sky and the water. Or you may see it at night as you look up into the sky – the corona borealis, the star-citadel of the exalted Lady of Light.

#  PRIESTESSES, POETS AND PROPHETS

## *GUARDIANS OF INNER SPACE*

The Irish and British Celtic pantheon contained many gods – Lleu, Manannan mac Llyr, Bran, Belenos, Cernunnos, the Dagda – and many goddesses – Arianrhod, Dana or Don, the Morrigan, Macha, Epona, to name a few at random. And while the Romans were in Western Europe many of their gods, notably Mars and Mercury, merged with the Celtic ones and were acknowledged by Romans and Celts alike. But according to archaeologist Miranda Green, what distinguished the Romano-Celtic religion from its purely Roman counterpart was the Celtic predilection for sacred couples – that is, a god and a goddess – working together.[16]

## SACRED COUPLES

Above: *Mercury and Rosmerta, a sacred couple, on a Gloucestershire stone tablet, third century* AD. (Craig Chapman)

Opposite: *The triple-goddess.*

At Bath the god Mars Loucetius ('brilliant') has a wholly Celtic consort, Nemetona. Both on the Continent and in England, we find Mercury paired with the Celtic Rosmerta ('the good purveyor'). On one stone tablet found in Gloucestershire he is portrayed with a caduceus, cockerel and purse, while she has a double axe in one hand and a patera and bucket in the other. On another tablet her head is shown as bigger than his, suggesting that she is the more important. Miranda Green comments that the female partners in these sacred couples are often purely Celtic, suggesting that the Celts were much more attached to the goddesses than the Romans were.

If we think of these pairs as tranquil married couples, we will get the wrong idea. The inherent dynamism of duality or polarity is expressed better in the kind of male–female conflicts we have already seen cropping up in the old myths and stories. Two is the number of opposition, dynamism, sexuality; the tension between two poles creates energy which can be used for creative purposes or to fuel the fires of war. The ability to 'bear the tension of the opposites', without giving in to war, was thought by C. G. Jung to be one of the most vital tasks of civilization. Often the male is operating in the outer world, insisting on the primacy of its values, while the female fights for the inner world and its different ethical claims.

70

This polarity is found, for instance, in the many different versions of the fairy-bride theme – a mortal man marries an Otherworld woman and she promises to bring him prosperity as long as he observes certain taboos. He breaks them and loses or perhaps destroys her and is himself broken-hearted (more about this in the next chapter).

As well as having a developed sense of polarity, of 'twoness', the Celts loved the number three: you find three wishes, three vows, three gods or goddesses cropping up everywhere in the mythologies. There is the triplicity of the Morrigan, Badb and Macha in Ireland, the three faces of Brigit – as patron of healing, poetry and smithcraft – the three matrones ('mothers') found in Romano-Celtic sculpture, and male threes as well: a triple Mars was found at Lower Slaughter in England and there is a Gaulish Mercury with a triple phallus; a three-faced stone head from around the first century BC was found in Sutherland in Scotland.[16]

Three is also a dynamic number, but it is more stable than two, having a quality of integrity and completeness; it contains energy more securely. You'll notice this if you are the witness in an argument between two people. Your presence, unless you take sides, may help to resolve the disagreement before it comes to blows or ends in unresolved antagonism.

Three is often associated with the three phases of the moon (waxing, full and waning, or new, crescent and full), or the three phases of a woman's life (maiden, mother and crone), or the 'three forces' of esoteric philosophy (active, receptive and unifying). In three the energy raised by two is resolved and 'held' in a kind of wholeness. In three we have the embodiment of

*Romano-Celtic sculpture of the Three Mothers, first century AD.*
(Craig Chapman)

72

differentiation within a unity, so that there is always a sense in which the 'three' is also a 'one'. Most religions and philosophical systems recognized the prime importance of the three, and the druids were no exception.

The druids were the acknowledged wise men of the Celts and had a network of influence stretching over all the Celtic lands, although Britain was said to be the centre for druidic education. The druidic training took twenty years, and we know that a large part of it consisted of learning material by heart. Even when the druids came into contact with the literate Roman culture, they forbade the writing down of their lore. In some parts of the Celtic world we know that women could become druids. In other places priestesses are referred to and they seem to have had a separate, perhaps complementary role.[2] We do not know exactly what the druidic metaphysical system was because we have only scraps of ancient lore and custom to go on, but it is useful for us to devise one of our own when thinking about Celtic religion, because otherwise it is difficult to make sense of the myriad gods, goddesses and half-way beings who float around, changing shape with every wind.

If we start out from our awareness that both two and three were important to the Celts, and then put the principle of duality together with the principle of triplicity, we either get this:

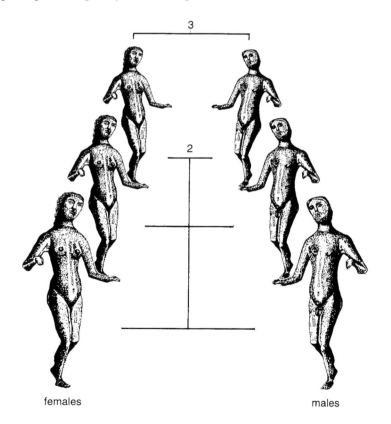

females                                                          males

which looks like three sets of couples facing each other in a dance, or this:

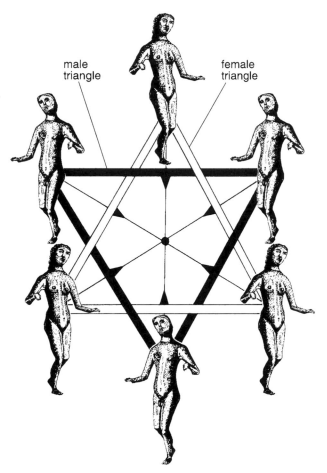

male
triangle

female
triangle

which sets the three couples opposite each other in a circle, and is immediately a more dynamic arrangement, because it also gives us a seventh point, the central one, which can be seen as a kind of spindle or nail around which the six move.

One of the simplest ways of dividing the gods and goddesses into a set of three pairs (in which the principle of two and the principle of three are both embodied) is to look for those associated with *light*, those associated with the *dark*, or the *underworld*, and those connected with *water*. We would then have a Lord and Lady of Light, a Lord and Lady of the Underworld and a Lord and Lady of the Waters. You will find that most gods and goddesses seem to fit into one of these categories, so that Arianrhod in her crystal castle is obviously a version of the Lady of Light, while Dana (Don in Wales), with her association with rivers, is a Lady of the Waters. The Morrigan who sits on battlefields in her crow-shape, picking at the bones of the dead, must belong to the underworld.

74

You can do the same for the gods of course, as here:

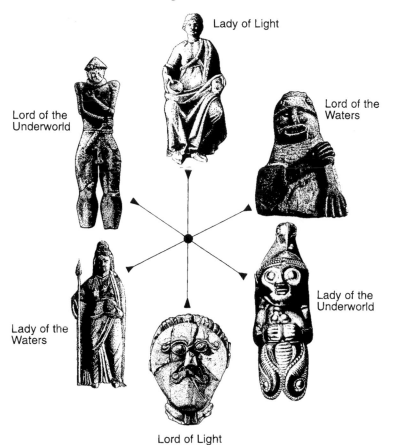

Lady of Light

Lord of the Underworld

Lord of the Waters

Lady of the Waters

Lady of the Underworld

Lord of Light

Below: *Silbury Hill, with swans at floodtime, evokes the presence of the Lady of the Waters.* (Cherry Gilchrist)

*The Lady of the Underworld. Her presence is felt inside the 5,000 year old New Grange tomb in County Meath, Ireland.*
(Craig Chapman)

Now we see the gods and goddesses standing opposite each other, ready to begin the dance of creation. Male and female power are equally balanced, the male embodying force and the female form, the male providing the energy while the female shapes it. The catch is that the female is the source of the energy in the first place, because, as Carlos Castaneda tells us in his books, 'the universe is female'.[17] If we think about the Irish ceremonies of kingship, where the goddess or priestess embodying 'sovereignty' gives the candidate ale to drink which symbolizes the power she has been keeping and guarding for him, we can see that the pagan Celts understood the basic principle of polarity very well. It is interesting that another traditional society, the Kogi people of Colombia, who consider themselves our 'elder brothers' and wish to lead us back from the brink of ecological disaster, also have a deep understanding of polarity, looking in everything that exists for its male and female aspects.[18]

The important thing about the pattern set out above is not to squeeze everything into it, as George Eliot's Mr Casaubon did with his 'Key to All Mythologies', but to use it to understand that gods and goddesses are living forces which always act together in relation to each other, as well as apparently alone. In this book we are concentrating on the female side of creation, but only because this has been hidden and neglected, not because it is superior to or more important than the male contribution.

# CELTIC PRIESTESSES

There are various Latin accounts of the existence and activities of Celtic priestesses. Pomponius Mela writes in the first century AD of a group of nine virgin priestesses who lived on the island of Sena off Cap du Raz, on the extreme southwestern tip of Brittany:

> they were reputed to have the power to unleash the winds and storms by their spells, to metamorphose into any animal according to their whim, to cure all diseases said to be incurable and, finally, to know and predict the future. But they reserved their remedies and predictions for those who had travelled over the seas expressly to consult them.

Nine is also a number beloved of the Celts, being of course an amplification of three – 3 × 3 – and is often particularly associated with women. Nine female magicians turn up in the Welsh tale of Peredur guarding the thermal waters of Gloucester and there are several stone circles in Britain which have nine 'female' stones, notably the Nine Ladies circle in Derbyshire. In the Arthurian cycle, Morgan le Fay is one of nine priestesses of Avalon who bear away the dying King Arthur to heal and conceal him until he is needed by Britain again.

It would obviously be useful to have specialists in weather-lore sitting just off such a notoriously stormy and dangerous coast, and being able to predict weather might look very like being able to control it. In western Scotland, there are tales still in currency of witches who could control the weather (see Chapter 7). The priestesses' shape-shifting abilities sound like a shamanic practice, and possibly this was the way they approached the curing

*The Nine Ladies stone circle, Derbyshire.*
(Craig Chapman)

77

of disease, using a form of shape-shifting magic such as you'll find today in some Native American Indian traditions. That the trip over to meet them was probably itself quite an ordeal in such tricky waters would also tend to put these women's clients into the kind of altered state of consciousness necessary to achieve such miracle cures.

Lastly, the fact that the women were virgins would have been seen to set them apart from ordinary women, whose lives would normally be given over to bearing and rearing children. The virgins would save their energy for their magical activities. Presumably they excited great awe and respect among the seafaring peoples who consulted them.

## THE BACCHANTES OF THE LOIRE

Late in the second century BC Posidonius reports that a group of women of the Namnetes tribe lived on a small island opposite the mouth of the Loire, practising what he called 'Bacchic' mysteries. No man was allowed to set foot on their island, but when they wanted to see their husbands the women would cross over to the mainland to do so. The most extraordinary element in the story is that once a year they would take the roof off their temple and cover it over again in the same day. If anyone let their bundle of materials fall to the ground, she was immediately torn to pieces by the others, who then carried her fragments around the temple with the cry of 'Evah!' The woman who was destined to be this sacrifice was supposedly jostled to make her drop her thatch.

These women were clearly using sexual energy to power up their activities; the yearly scapegoat may be seen as a safety valve without whom riot would ensue. Or perhaps the threat of this terrible fate simply existed to keep the priestesses awake and on their toes. We do not know whether the killing actually happened or was simply a rumour put about by people who feared the women of the island.

In Greece the 'Bacchic' rites at one time would have involved a group of ecstatic, intoxicated women tearing apart an animal (or even a man) with their bare hands and eating it. This is the kind of pagan practice which we find difficult to understand today, even though the drinking of Christ's blood in the Christian mass is an echo of such ceremonies, where the 'sacrifice' is 'eaten' by the congregation who thereby participate in Christ's holy essence.

Reports such as these are useful to dwell on if we feel like romanticizing the Celts. Some scholars do not believe that human sacrifice was an essential part of Celtic society; others claim that the druids sacrificed frequently, and cite classical reports of the 'bloodstained altars' of Anglesey and references to sacrifice for divinatory purposes. We have only to remember what Boudicca did in Andraste's name to the Roman women of London (see

*Fedelm, the poet-prophet.*

78

Chapter 6) to realize that Celtic women did not lag behind their men in bloodthirstiness.

However, almost all early pagan civilizations had practices which seem cruel to us now. The 'civilized' Romans, who claimed to be appalled by the druid sacrifices, were quite happy to watch both Christian and non-Christian gladiators die horribly in the arena (avoid reading the eyewitness accounts unless you have a very strong stomach). Our appetite for blood in Western Europe is still keen, but we usually satisfy it indirectly via films and television now – take, for example, the popularity of films like *Pulp Fiction*.

## FEDELM THE POET AND PROPHET

Islands of wise or sacred women are a frequent theme of early Irish literature (see Chapter 6), but there were also loners such as the poet-prophet Fedelm, who meets with Maeve in the *Tain*. She is described as young and very beautiful: 'She had hair in three tresses: two wound upward on her head, the third hanging down her back, brushing her calves. She held a light gold weaving rod in her hand, with gold inlay. Her eyes had triple irises. Two black horses drew her chariot and she was armed.'[9]

The three tresses and the triple irises in her eyes may be special signs of her profession, the sacred three again. The weaving rod sounds like a magical instrument, referring to the idea, found in many ancient cultures, that there are three fey women who weave the fate of worlds and humans. It may also symbolize the clarity of vision of one who *weaves threads* rather than *is woven* herself into the cloth, meaning that Fedelm is a woman in control of her own destiny. Lastly, the fact that she is armed marks her out as a free woman who may go where she wishes and need fear no one. Certainly she shows no fear of Maeve, even though what she has to say can hardly please the wily queen.

> 'Where have you come from?' Maeve asked.
> 'From learning verse and vision in Alba,' the girl said.
> 'Have you the *imbas forasnai*, the Light of Foresight?' Maeve said.
> 'Yes, I have.'
> 'Then look for me and see what will become of my army.' So the girl looked.
> Maeve said, 'Fedelm, prophetess, how seest thou the host?'
> Fedelm said in reply: 'I see it crimson, I see it red.'
> 'That can't be true,' Maeve said.[9]

Although Maeve persists in refusing to face the fact that her troops are doomed, Fedelm sticks to her guns and keeps repeating her prophecy. In fact, she draws a clear picture of the victory of Cuchulain and the 'torn corpses and women wailing' which will result from the fray. She refuses to give Maeve the comforting news of her own success that she would like to hear.

The skill of prophecy or the 'second sight' persists up to this day in the Highlands and islands of Scotland (see Chapter 7) and was cunningly preserved when Christianity arrived by being ascribed to Mary and Brigit: the *frith Mhoire* was the augury of Mary. One poem tells of how Mary used it to find out where the child Jesus had gone when he was disputing with the rabbis of the temple.[19] When seeking a lost person or possession, the seer would make a tube of her palms and looking down it would *see* the whereabouts of that which was lost. This was the *imbas forasnai* which Scathach possessed (see Chapter 7) and which Fedelm went to learn about in Alba.

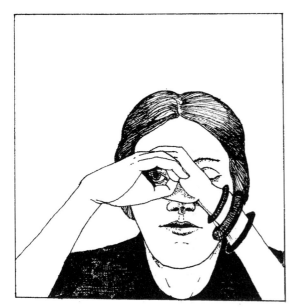

*A woman practising 'imbas forasnai', the Light of Foresight.* (Craig Chapman)

## The Innkeeper Prophet

**f**LAVIUS Vopiscus writes that Gaius Aurelius Diocletian, while still a humble soldier, was settling his bill at an inn in Gaul when his hostess pulled him up on his meanness in haggling about the amount. 'I'd be a lot freer with my money if I were the emperor,' he said. The landlady replied, 'Laugh not, Diocletian, for when you have slain the boar, you will indeed be emperor.' Diocletian later rose in rank and slew the prefect Arrius, whose nickname was 'the Boar', and became emperor of Rome. Unfortunately he was a cruel persecutor of Christians, but the innkeeper-prophet was accurate in her prediction.[2]

# BRIGIT – THE MARY AND THE JUNO OF THE GAELS

The most famous Celtic priestess of all is St Brigit, still one of the best loved of Irish saints, along with St Patrick. It is said that her nuns kept the sacred fire burning at Kildare from the beginning of her rule there as Abbess in AD 490 until it was extinguished briefly by order of the Archbishop of Dublin in 1220. No man was allowed to enter the sanctuary – a sacred area marked out by a hedge – which was tended by some say nine, others nineteen, nuns.

Kildare is in Irish Cill Dara, meaning the church of the oak wood, and oaks were usually associated with druids. Evidence suggests that there was a pre-Christian shrine here for some time before St Brigit came on the scene, probably sacred to the goddess Brigit or Brig. We know that some plains in the area were left untilled even though fertile, a sign that the goddess owned them.[20] So it is likely that a group of priestesses lived in or near Kildare and performed the rites associated with Brigit as a fertility goddess.

What might these rites have been? Barbara Walker[21] suggests that these women may have been sacred harlots, offering themselves as representatives of the Goddess in rites to ensure the fertility of the land. She describes how 'holy virgin' was the title of the harlot-priestesses of Ishtar, Asherah or Aphrodite in cultures further east.

Their functions were to heal, to prophesy, to perform sacred dances, to wail for the dead and to become brides of God (or the god). Children born of these women were called by the Greeks *parthenoi*, 'virgin-born'. They were regarded as children of the god, not children of men. The 'magical' baby boys who appear frequently in Celtic mythology, who are supposed to have gods for fathers, may well have been conceived in such temples.

Esther Harding, in her book *Women's Mysteries*, mentions the association of fire with the fertilizing principle and describes how the rite of *hieros gamos* (sacred marriage) would have been performed in these Mediterranean societies:

> In the mysteries, the chief priestess, who impersonated the Moon Goddess, herself was 'married' once a year, to a man impersonating the male principle, the Priapic God. While the mystery was enacted in the holy place, the worshippers kept vigil in the temple. At the consummation of the rite attendant priestesses came forth from the sacred shrine bearing the new Sacred Fire which had just been born through the renewal of the power of the goddess, and from the new fire the household fires of all the worshippers were relighted.[22]

Given the Celtic feeling for polarity, it is very possible that a similar rite was performed at Brigit's shrine, and is the origin of the custom of keeping

*Brigit, the Mary and the Juno of the Gael.*

83

the sacred fire alight. There is some suggestive evidence to support this from Scotland, where Brigit is called Bride and there are many customs still remembered which celebrate her feast day, which is on the same day as the Celtic feast of Imbolc on 1 February. (Imbolc marks the beginning of spring and the first lactation of the ewes.) We should bear in mind the very strong connection between Ireland and western Scotland during Celtic times: in the early Dark Ages settlers from northeast Ireland actually came over to what is now Argyllshire and settled there. This became the kingdom of Dalriada. Therefore these customs may well have come originally from rites associated with Brigit in Ireland.

The Bride figure which the young maidens of the Highlands carried from door to door was, of course, the Christianized St Brigit, although the way they decked the figure with shining shells, sparkling crystals, primroses, snowdrops and greenery makes it sound very much like the image of a spring goddess – you can almost smell the rain on her leaves! After making a round of the village, the girls would go to a house to make the Bride feast. Marian McNeill, quoting an earlier folklorist, Alexander Carmichael, describes it thus:

> They bar the door and secure the windows of the house, and set Bride where she may see and be seen by all. Presently the young men of the community come humbly asking permission to honour Bride. After some parleying they are admitted and make obeisance to her.
>
> Much dancing and singing, fun and frolic are indulged in during the night. As the grey dawn of the Day of Bride breaks they form a circle and sing the hymn, 'Beauteous Bride, Choice Foster Mother of Christ'. They then distribute the fragments of the feast among the poor women of the place.[6]

The way the house is at first shut up protectively, like a guarded secret, is a symbol of Bride's and her young acolytes' virginity. When the boys come 'humbly asking permission to honour Bride', they feel very much like young aspirants come to worship the goddess prior to being initiated into her secrets via the act of sacred sexual intercourse. That ecstatic intercourse is symbolized in this 'respectable' Christian rite by the way the boys are finally allowed to enter the closed house and enjoy themselves all night, dancing and singing.

The association of Bride with the snake is also suggestive. In the Highlands this hymn was sung:

> Today is the day of Bride;
> The serpent shall come from the hole,
> I will not molest the serpent
> Nor will the serpent molest me.[6]

If we take the serpent to be a phallic symbol, or at least an embodiment of unregenerate sexual energy, then it seems as if there is something about Bride which neutralizes the threat of that. In the Christian version the serpent must be destroyed – Marian McNeill tells a nice story of a respectable Scottish matron rising up from the fireside on Bride's day, taking off her stocking and filling it with peat and then pounding it with the fire tongs while intoning these words:

> This is the day of Bride:
> The queen will come from the mound;
> I will not touch the queen
> Nor will the queen touch me.

Is the 'queen' a fairy woman from a fairy mound, associated with the serpent, and standing in for the old goddess Brigit, who performed the old sexual rites which must now be suppressed? The earthy pagan fertility goddess has now to be separated from the pure and holy saint . . . and yet the little rhyme recognizes their connection. The pagan Brigit's vast energies are now put to use in the minding of cows, the caring for women in childbirth and the succouring of the poor and the weak, rather than in securing the fertility of the land via some variety of sacred marriage.

Indeed, in the figure of the Christian Brigit perhaps we find one of the secrets of the enormous appeal of Christianity to the Irish and Scottish people in those early years of Patrick and Brigit: it transformed the fierce and demanding face of the Goddess, who would sometimes grant favour and sometimes deny it, into the sweet face of a motherly saint who would always do her best for humankind. As Norah Jones points out, the Scottish Gaels wove Bride into the very fabric of the Bible stories, so as to be able to retain their deep affection for her.

> The story goes that Bride was in Bethlehem at the inn when Mary and Joseph came asking for shelter. She had to tell them the inn was full but gave them some water from her own jug, and a piece of her own bannock. After they left she saw that the water-jug was full and the bannock whole again. Then she went to the stable, where she arrived in time to receive the infant Jesus in her arms as he was born, thus gaining her role as midwife to Mary and foster mother to Christ.[19]

*Stone carving of the goddess Brigantia, forerunner of St Brigit, from Birrens, Dumfriesshire, circa second century AD.*
(Craig Chapman)

## The Pagan Brigit

In pre-Christian times Brigit or Brig or Brigantia was worshipped all over Europe. Her name means 'exalted one'. A federation of tribes called the Brigantes, named after her, lived in the northwest of Britain. In Ireland she was the patroness of poetry, healing and smithcraft, three areas which can

85

actually be assigned to the categories of Light, Waters and Underworld. Poetry is to do with inspiration, which comes 'in a flash of lightning'; healing is often associated with water – consider all the healing wells and the idea of 'streams of living water'; smithcraft, the moulding of iron which comes out of the earth with fire, is an underworldish kind of craft. In fact she embodied all three aspects of the Goddess in her person. She was also said to be variously the wife, daughter or mother of the great god Dagda, so she was clearly associated with the Tuatha De Danann, the skilful, wise and magical race who retreated into the fairy mounds when defeated by the Fomoire. Her imagery, according to Mary Condren, was associated with the sun, moon, cows, sheep, vultures, baths, sacred fires, serpents and milk.[23]

## St Brigit

There are many tales and sayings about St Brigit, but no one is sure that she ever actually existed. If she did, she is thought to have died about AD 524, and the first written references to her begin around the year AD 600. One account says her father was a druid, Dubtach, and her mother a slave, which is one way of obliquely recognizing her pagan origins. The first *Life of Brigit*, written by the monk Cogitosus, contained lots of miracles but no facts. However, the miracles are interesting because they begin to build up the image of Brigit which has lasted to the present day – as a woman of extraordinary kindness and purity of heart who also possesses amazing magical powers. As a girl she gives away the butter she has churned to the poor, but God replenishes it; she is able to hang her wet clothes on a sunbeam to dry; she changes water into ale for lepers; she produces a convenient miscarriage for a nun who has strayed. Behind the mask of the perfect saint, though, there sometimes stirs the breath of a woman of flesh and blood.

### Brigit and the Dumb Girl

COGITOSUS tells the story of a woman who brings her dumb daughter to Brigit for healing. Brigit asks the 12-year-old girl, 'Do you want to marry or be a nun?'
Immediately the mother breaks in and says,
'She won't answer, you know!'
Whereupon Brigit takes the child's hand and says she won't let it go until she answers. The girl soon blurts out,
'I don't want anything except what you want!'

We sense in this story about Brigit a keen sensitivity to other people's emotions. She must have realized that she had to break the girl's bond with her mother (possibly one which was holding her back) by making a physical bond with her which would give her a 'way out' from her presumably self-induced dumbness. This sounds like the kind of 'miracle' we can still accept today, based as it is on a sound understanding of human nature.

## Brigit and the Soul-friend

Another story shows the same kind of awareness, this time sharpened to the point of clairvoyance. It comes from a ninth-century text supposedly written by the monk Oengus mac Oengoban. In those days in the Celtic Church it was thought necessary for every monk or nun to have an *amchara*, a 'soul-friend', someone with whom he or she could discuss their spiritual progress and to whom they could confess their sins — a bit like a confessor, only an equal.

'Well, young cleric there,' says Brigit, 'hast thou a soul-friend?'

'I have,' replied the young cleric.

'Let us sing his requiem,' says Brigit, 'for he has died. I saw when half thy portion had gone that thy quota was put into thy trunk, and thou without any head on thee, for thy soul-friend died and anyone without a soul-friend is a body without a head, and eat no more until thou gettest a soul-friend.'[20]

It would seem that Brigit *saw* a vision which told her that this young man's soul-friend had died just as Fedelm *saw* the colour red which signified the defeat of Maeve's armies. Brigit here is clearly carrying on a tradition of clairvoyance and prophecy from her pre-Christian sisters. Scholar Whitley Stokes summed up some of the lore about Brigit thus:

> Brigit was born at sunrise neither within nor without a house, was bathed in milk, her breath revives the dead, a house in which she is staying flames up to heaven, cow-dung blazes before her, oil is poured on her head; she is fed from the milk of a white red-eared cow; a fiery pillar rises over her head; sun rays support her wet cloak; she remains a virgin; and she was one of the two mothers of Christ the Anointed.[20]

Remember Lleu, the magical boy from the story of Arianrhod? Well, Brigit shares his quality of having one foot in heaven and one on earth, being born at the time when night becomes day, neither indoors nor outdoors. The paradoxes noted by Stokes (house burns without consuming Brigit, she is a virgin and yet a mother) are signs of a person who can move into the higher realm where apparent contradictions are resolved, a liminal being who can travel between the worlds and therefore perform miracles.

## *Brigit and Kildare*

The description of the church which St Brigit established at Kildare is interesting. It contained two doors, one through which the monks of her community entered, plus the men and boys of the locality, and another through which the nuns and women came in. They were then seated on either side of the church, separated by an aisle. This separation of the sexes should not be seen as insulting to women; what we have here again is the old Celtic understanding of the power of polarity, and you cannot have polarity without separation. Brigit knew that this set-up in church would generate energy for prayer, and her abbey, like many others established by women in the early days of Christianity in both Ireland and England, had religious people of both sexes in it. Brigit was in charge, although she did arrange for Archbishop Conleth to come and look after the men, while she took care of the women.

Kildare was a refuge, a place of sanctuary, and it is perhaps the memory of this that lingers in the beautiful hymns to Bride, which come from Scotland.

> I shall not be killed,
> I shall not be harried,
> I shall not be put in cell,
> I shall not be wounded,
> Neither shall Christ leave me in forgetfulness,
> No fire, no sun, no moon shall burn me,
> No water, no loch, no sea shall drown me,
> No arrow of fairy or dart of fay shall wound me,
> And I under the protection of Holy Mary,
> And my gentle foster mother, my beloved Bride.[11]

Here is Brigit in her role as foster mother who will let nothing harm her children. Note that this hymn is not strictly speaking a prayer but more a kind of incantation. Brigit is one of the main channels by which our pagan past flows harmoniously into our Christian and post-Christian present.

However, Brigit as either goddess or saint could not halt the gradual slide of the Irish Christian Church away from its Celtic form, in which women could have and hold power, into the Romanized version, where they were considered inferior. Mary Condren points to three symbolic incidents in this degeneration. First, in AD 888 the Irish annals record that for the first time virgins cut their hair. Since hair in the old religions of Europe had always been a living symbol of women's power, this act clearly marked the fading of that power. Then in 1132 the Abbess of Kildare, Brigit's successor, was raped by the troops of King Dermot mac Murrough, a Leinster king who wanted to make her unfit for her post so that he could install his own candidate. Lastly, when the sacred fire was extinguished in 1220, that could have been the end of Kildare if the local people had not risen up and demanded that it be relit. But although Brigit's abbey at Kildare did survive this insult, it languished in relative obscurity until finally snuffed out in the suppression of the monasteries in 1540.[23]

However, maybe the story is not as depressing as it sounds. We can have faith that women within the Christian Church have kept that sacred fire lit, in their hearts if not in the physical sense, by being aware of their connection back into time with all women who have guarded the sacred fires of creation, whether Christian or pagan. In fact, in 1993, the nuns of the Brigidine Order in Kildare relit the sacred flame, and it now burns day and night in a quiet room in the ordinary house where they live. A house visited by people like Clare O'Grady Walsh, director of Greenpeace in Ireland, Sinead O'Connor the passionate singer, and women from all over Europe, Australia and New Zealand drawn by the name of Brigit. Fire from the flame was taken via London to the International Women's Conference in Beijing in August 1995. Who knows what those strong, determined Catholic women in their sensible chain-store skirts and blouses have started? Maybe they have been the secret guardians of the Goddess all along!

## Brigit and the Priestesses

To understand what priestesshood meant to the Celts, we need to look a bit more closely at the meaning of the sacred fire and why it had to be guarded by women. In Rome six Vestal Virgins tended the fire which symbolized the spirit of Rome. If they let it go out, they were flogged; if they lost their virginity, they were locked in an underground chamber to starve to death. So, their virginity was felt to be even more important than the flame. It is typical of the Romans to make something spiritual as material as they could.

If you have ever visited a shrine or temple where a sacred flame has been burning for a long time, you may have noticed the extraordinary atmosphere it creates, as if all the restless impurities in the air have been burnt away, leaving a great, profound peace. The flame makes the space holy; it symbolizes the divine itself, while its corona and the purified air around it are the presence of the divine. In Jewish mysticism this presence is known as the *shekina* and is sometimes identified with *sophia*, the wisdom of God. Therefore the job of the priestesses who work in such a temple is to protect that divine essence and presence, to make a space for it to exist in the world and be witnessed by humankind. Because we are dealing here with the pristine beginnings of things, the moment of conception if you like, it is important that those priestesses embody within themselves a space which is inviolate and pure. This is not moral logic at all but symbolic logic; it does not say virginity is ethically desirable, simply that it is necessary to do this job.

But what, you may ask, about the sacred harlots? They represent a different sort of priestess, she who participates in the sacred marriage and in whose body a conception may occur which will result in the birth of a magical or holy child. If we see the virgins as celebrating the moment just before creation, the harlots can be seen as celebrating the ecstasy of the union itself, a moment which comes slightly later. A religion may choose either or perhaps both ways of doing it. Or, as in the Christian Church, it may sublimate the sexual to the point that no woman is actually involved in its rites.

Both virgin priestesses and sacred harlots are guardians of inner space, the space in which the act of creation happens. Ordinary people often pick up strongly on their protective quality, which is why Brigit has become such a comforting and popular saint, but priestesses must also be capable of ruthless objectivity, the clarity which can see the essence of truth under its clothing. People often call this kind of clarity clairvoyance.

*St Catherine's Chapel, Abbotsbury, Dorset – a beacon belonging to the Lady of the Light.* (Lyn Webster Wilde)

If you want to visit a site where priestesses of the Lady of Light may have worked, go to Abbotsbury in Dorset (by coincidence, the place where the colour paintings for this book were created!) and if possible walk into the village, from the inland hills towards the sea, just as the sun is setting.

You will see a strange hill with a serpentine spiral winding round it, upon which stands the Abbey of St Catherine. The next morning climb the hill and visit the abbey. If the sun is shining and the air is crystalline, it will be easy to sense the blessed atmosphere which the priestesses worked to create. As a building, the abbey is not particularly impressive, but you will be able to feel the presence of the Lady in it nevertheless.

St Catherine is another one of those saints who may never have existed, but she is a friend to all women and the patron saint of both spinsters and sailors, supposedly being able to find husbands for the former and, via her beacons of fire, save the latter from shipwreck. The emperor who wanted to marry her had her tortured to death on the wheel – hence the Catherine wheel, one of the most spectacular fireworks there is – but a bolt of lightning saved her from that particular form of death. When she was beheaded, milk spurted from her body rather than blood, a curious link with her sister light-bearer Brigit.[21] The wheel, of course, links her with Arianrhod, whose 'starry wheel' or revolving castle is a palace of light.

# QUEENS OF TWO WORLDS

## BRITISH QUEENS

Tacitus wrote that it was not an unusual occurrence for the British to be ruled by a woman, and indeed in the British Isles there is a tradition of strong assertive female leadership. Queens Elizabeth I and Victoria are the shining stars of the second half of the millennium, but the precedent for toughness was set 1500 years before Elizabeth lived, by Boudicca and Cartimandua, Celtic rulers in the critical period when Britain was struggling against the Roman invaders. Here is how Dio Cassius describes Boudicca:

> In stature she was very tall, in appearance most terrifying, in the glance of her eye most fierce, and her voice was harsh; a great mass of the tawniest hair fell to her hips; around her neck was a large golden necklace; and she wore a tunic of divers colours over which a thick mantle was fastened with a brooch. This was her invariable attire.

When we read the above passage, are we reading about the real Boudicca? The historian Dio Cassius was born 100 years after she lived and no eyewitness accounts remain of this, the most famous British heroine of all time. Although there is no question that she actually existed, leading the armies of the Iceni into battle against the Romans, everything else about her has the larger-than-life quality of myth. We have no way of knowing whether any of it is true or not.

However, it is true that along with King Arthur and Merlin, Boudicca (whose name means 'victory') is one of the makers of the national identity of Britain. The person who nearly managed to drive the Romans from Celtic Britain was not a heroic, battle-hardened general but a widowed woman who stepped into the breach because necessity demanded it. That we still have in these lands a firm acceptance of female rule, be it by our two Elizabeths and our sturdy Victoria or by our admired and hated Prime Minister Thatcher, may be partly due to the tradition kept alive by Boudicca in the dark times which form a bridge between the ancient matri-centred world of Europe and our own queasy quasi-feminist times.

In the year AD 60 the lands we now call Norfolk and northern Suffolk were occupied by the Iceni. Their king, Prasutagus, had been one of those pragmatic rulers who had decided to co-operate with the Romans and become a 'client king', in return for retaining his own position and power. Now he had died and left his estate for the Roman emperor and his daughters to share, hoping that this compromise would keep the peace.

## Boudicca's Humiliation

'TOO OLD and plain to rape,' that's what they said, the day they came to take her and her daughters away. She didn't need mastery of their alien tongue to know that's what they were laughing about as they ripped her dress down off her shoulders and tied her hands to the post ready for the flogging. Her people stood around behind the cohorts of Roman soldiers watching. Their faces were impassive and they kept absolute silence. The soldiers were uncomfortable. They would have much preferred the usual Celtic wailing and screeching – then they could have stepped in and applied the heavy hand to the situation.

But her people, the Iceni, knew to save their energy – and their voices – for what was to come. As for Boudicca herself, she barely felt the bite of the rods on the flesh of her back and shoulders: her whole body hummed with rage, a rage so incandescent it felt as cold as ice. She sensed because she neither screamed nor begged for mercy that the soldiers beating her were not enjoying themselves. She had been trained by the priestesses of her sisterhood in the technique of self-control. That was what lay behind the appearance of superhuman courage, and it would create a useful reputation for her in the days to come.

She did not feel brave when she thought about what they were doing to her little girls, only 12 and 13, not even marriageable yet, but what did the Romans care about women's suffering? They kept their own women shut up in their homes like slaves and she'd heard that the executioners raped little virgins before killing them because it was considered unlucky to kill a virgin . . . But at least her darlings were not being outraged in public, and at least they would not be killed. She bore it by thinking of her revenge: what she would do to the Roman women when she was the victor and they were the losers, as they would surely be.

After the flogging and the raping, they were given their clothes back and told to go home. She sensed the uneasiness of some of the soldiers. They had not been allowed to enjoy themselves in the usual war-footing sort of way. She guessed they had been told to be restrained and use minimum force: this was to be a symbolic rape and flogging, designed to break the spirit of the natives by making them witness the public humiliation of their queen, not to make a bloody mess or cause a public disturbance. The gods forbid!

The girls were dry-eyed, of course. They too had had the training. As they walked to their waiting chariot, Boudicca whispered to them, 'Straight backs! And don't let them catch your eyes, keep your eyes forward or they'll get the hooks of humiliation into you!'

The situation was this: the greedy Roman finance minister, Catus Decianus, had not respected the terms of Prasutagus's will. He had taken all his lands and goods on behalf of the emperor, had ordered the ritual humiliation of the king's wife and daughters, and had helped himself on Rome's behalf to the lands belonging to the nobles of the tribe. Now, on the way home to the ransacked royal house, Queen Boudicca made her vows: she vowed to the goddess Andraste that she would revenge this insult. The Romans would find that the same woman they had flogged like a slave would become a figurehead behind which the Iceni and other angry tribes would gather; the arrogant Romans' final humiliation should be that a woman had destroyed them.

## The First Battle

CAMULODUNUM (Colchester) was, in AD 61, already an established Roman town, the centre of Roman government in Britain. The inhabitants were so confident that their prosperity would last that they had built no walls to protect themselves. Generous grants of land snatched from the native tribes had drawn army veterans to the area. They imported Mediterranean dates and figs and wine. An enormous and grandiose new temple to the Emperor Claudius had been built. They were utterly unprepared for Boudicca's attack.

Before setting out on the campaign the queen had sought auguries from Andraste, the Goddess of War, by letting a hare sacred to the goddess run out from the folds of her robes. It had taken the auspicious direction, so Boudicca's troops went into battle knowing they would be victorious. It was, in fact, an easy victory. Some brave Romans holed up for two days in the temple, waiting for reinforcements, but these never came and they perished, along with all the rest of the citizens.

The town itself was burnt to the ground, but only after the decapitated heads of the slain enemy had been paraded around the temple precincts. Boudicca was pleased, but this was only a beginning. Her 120,000 warriors, plus the wagons with their wives and children and supplies, began to trundle across the countryside, laying waste to any Roman or pro-Roman settlements they came across on the way. They had not known that victory could be so easy.

*Boudicca, warrior queen of the Iceni.*

## Boudicca's Antagonist

UETONIUS Paulinus was 60 years old and had been appointed military governor of Britain in AD 59. He had fought the natives of both Spain and Gaul and was used to campaigning in mountainous territory. While Boudicca sacked Camulodunum he had been dealing with the rebel stronghold of Mona (Anglesey) and the druids who had their centre there. The last battle had been a gruesome affair – lines of black-clad women, with limed hair sticking up from their heads like spears, threading their way sinuously through the ranks of warriors screeching and ululating, and circles of druid priests reaching up into the skies and calling on their gods to destroy the Roman soldiers as they waited to fight. It was like a visitation from the underworld and at first Suetonius's troops were paralysed with dread. But the old general had seen this sort of thing before; to him it was simply cheap magic designed to disorder the senses and weaken the resolve. He had stronger magic. He told his men to ignore the racket and concentrate their minds solely on the job in hand. The men had great faith in the old warhorse. The fact that he was entirely unmoved by their enemy's uncanny tricks settled their nerves. They marched forward and efficiently slaughtered the Celts and their weird women, and then they moved in to cut down the sacred groves and bloodstained altars of these barbarian priests.

Now messengers had arrived to tell Suetonius about Boudicca's campaign. She was believed to be heading towards Londinium (London), a fair-sized Roman settlement of 30,000 souls. Would the general return to the south immediately to protect the emperor's possessions there – and his citizens, of course? Suetonius marched to Londinium, where he made camp and pondered. Boudicca must be stopped. In spite of his recent tactical victory over the druids, known to be the spiritual leaders of the Celtic people, he knew that the balance of power in Britain was still precarious. The Britons were reckless and supernaturally brave. They did not need to be paid to fight, like his own soldiers, they went into battle half-naked, with nothing but their writhing tattoos and ornamental shields for protection, and they genuinely did not fear to die. He felt this gave them a certain edge!

Suetonius decided to sacrifice Londinium. His men were too few to defend it. They would not be eager to die in a blaze of glory in the manner of the Celt and must live to fight another day. Whoever among the inhabitants could get out of Londinium did so, leaving all those who could not keep up with the soldiers to their fate.

As for Boudicca, she was no tactician. She wanted vengeance and her troops wanted blood and booty. They were more than pitiless in their actions. The most noble women were stripped and hung on the walls; their breasts were cut off and sewn into their mouths so that they appeared to

*Roman head, thought to be Emperor Claudius.* (British Museum)

be eating them. Or they were impaled lengthways on sharp skewers. Boudicca and her daughters watched with sharp excitement and enjoyment. Although they were women, they could rape too, through the agency of iron. Andraste was satisfied, her thirst for blood finally sated by her priestess's skill. While Londinium's citizens shrieked in an agony of slow death, the Iceni and their allies looted, feasted and drank deep of the fine wines they had found. Then Londinium was reduced to ashes, as Camulodunum had been.

The Iceni's third victory was at Verulanium (St Albans). Here the inhabitants had more time to flee, so that the destruction was less bloody, but they were mainly Britons who were on the side of Rome, so they can have expected no pity from Boudicca's forces if they were caught.

With three victories under their belts, the Iceni felt invincible. When Suetonius finally decided he had no choice but to take them on, they were so confident of success that they allowed their wives and children to sit round in a semicircle on top of the wagons and watch. But Suetonius, the rational man, had chosen a good site for the battle, where the Iceni were squeezed between two pieces of high ground, while the Romans had tree-cover and high ground behind them. He was vastly outnumbered but his troops were well armed, skilful and battle-hardened.

Before the battle Boudicca rode around in her chariot, spear in hand, speaking to every clan, reminding them that she was not just their queen and commander, but a woman whose body had borne the marks of the lash, whose daughters had been violated by these invading fiends. She knew that if the men did not want to fight, then the women would, because they would know how she, as a woman and a mother, must feel.

The Romans found her voice harsh, but speaking to her own people it was soft, though clear as a bell. They would die for her; she was ready to die for them – they were kin, branches of the same tree. But they would not have to die, because the ferocious goddess Andraste was on their side . . .

Suetonius watched contemptuously. 'There are more women than men fighting in their army,' he drawled. In fact, there were only a handful of young female warriors in the British ranks, but the men's long hair and love of gold adornment made many of them as beautiful as girls.

The Roman foot soldiers prayed to their own gods as they advanced on the shrieking barbarians, but it was the units of cavalry on each wing that really helped them. As they pushed forward, the horsemen were able to stop the British from spreading out on to the high ground. They were squeezed back between the two hills and crowded up together so that they could not use their chariots or their long swords in the usual way. Thus hampered, they tried to retreat but found themselves hemmed in by their own wagons. Some of the women and children, seeing the way the battle was going, ran away, but most stayed, joined the fight with whatever makeshift weapons they could lay hands on and were slaughtered, along with the oxen that had pulled the wagons.

About 80,000 Britons fell that day. Over the period of the rebellion 150,000 people were slaughtered in all. It is said that Boudicca herself survived the battle but drank poison – and presumably shared it with her daughters – before she could be taken prisoner. She did not wish to travel to Rome in chains to feature in Suetonius's victory celebrations. Suetonius was bitterly disappointed that she had slipped through his fingers.

It seemed as if, on her death, the goddess Andraste had switched sides and made him her servant instead. He had the British prisoners dispatched with utmost savagery and then led his troops around the countryside on a campaign of brutal repression dedicated to Mars Ulator, the god of vengeance.

Andraste smiled. She did not care which side gave her blood to drink and entrails to chew, or to whom Suetonius thought he was dedicating the slaughter. The troops continued to kill, burn and pillage until a gentler procurator was appointed. The Romans were to rule in Britain for another 400 years. [24,25]

Boudicca would have been in her thirties or forties when the campaign took place, having probably married Prasutagus in her mid-teens. The two daughters may have been all the family she had left, boys having died or been killed in battle, or she may have had only the two children. In this case, it is possible that she did have some sort of warrior training herself. I would speculate that among the Celts aggressive, athletic girls may have been allowed to train with the boys and perhaps when they married they would keep their families small, to preserve their strength and energy for battle. Otherwise, Boudicca would have learned her battle skills by watching. Certainly, several of the classical accounts of Celtic war practices tell how the women would stand on the sidelines and support the men by terrifying enemies with their weird war-calls and outrageous demeanour.

The episode with the hare sacred to Andraste suggests that the queen may also have been a priestess, and if she was, this would have helped her weld together her enormous rabble of warriors into a unified force. The hare was considered a taboo animal by the Celts – that is, it was never eaten. Later, we know, it was associated with the moon, with fertility and witches, so it is clearly an animal linked to the idea of female power, and therefore would have had a close connection with Boudicca herself. The ritual may have been devised by her and her druid advisers as an effective piece of theatre, to help the people transfer their allegiance to a female ruler. It may also explain the particular atrocities inflicted on the Roman women of London; perhaps those who had affronted the goddess of war and her

*Hare in stone carving from Aquae Sulis, Bath, third century AD.*
(Craig Chapman)

priestess had to be punished by having their womanhood desecrated in a specific manner. There is a possibility, of course, that these tortures never happened and were made up by Roman propagandists to justify their own subsequent harshness.

In spite of this cruelty (and I think we have to accept it as part of Boudicca's nature and the customs of the times, not seek to excuse it or diminish it), Boudicca emerges as a courageous and spirited woman. The Romans were very shaken indeed by the rebellion and Emperor Nero almost decided to pull out of the island.

Cartimandua, however, seems to have operated on the other side in the battle between Britons and Romans. The detail of her story, shown opposite, comes mainly from Tacitus.

Cartimandua and Boudicca come over as very different kinds of queen. Although Cartimandua was ruthless and clear-headed, she preferred honourable surrender to battle to the death and thus bought many years of relative peace and prosperity for her people. We find her betrayal of Caratacus as difficult to swallow as we do Boudicca's atrocious cruelty to the Roman women, but we have to acknowledge that, having made a decision to co-operate with the Romans, Cartimandua could hardly back out of it without seeing herself and her kingdom destroyed.

She may have been the kind of queen who puts the day-to-day welfare of her people before their honour. Maybe she did not think it mattered who was keeping an eye on her, whether it was the male elders of the Brigantes or the Roman elders. Maybe she enjoyed the power of rulership and wanted to hold on to it at all costs. Maybe she felt herself to be part of a long line of female rulers who were pragmatic rather than principled in their methods – Queen Maeve of Connacht was certainly of this ilk! – and Cartimandua could well have been of Irish stock, living within easy enough reach of that island.

100

## Cartimandua, Queen of the Brigantes

CARTIMANDUA'S position as queen of the Brigantes was precarious. When Claudius led the big Roman push into Britain in AD 43 he ended by taking much of the south and midlands under direct rule, while allowing certain other areas to become client kingdoms, ruled independently but with allegiance to Rome. After one bitter battle, this is what happened to the northern kingdom of the Brigantes. The ringleaders of the resistance were killed but otherwise there were no reprisals. However, there were many of her people, Cartimandua's consort, Venutius, among them, who wanted the tribes of the Brigantes to continue to resist Roman rule. There were others who did not like being ruled by a woman. When people said to them, 'But it's a tradition in our country to have female rulers from time to time,' they would reply, 'When they're made of the same mettle as men, why not? But this one, she's more interested in a good time in bed than the welfare of her people.'

In fact, Cartimandua was perfectly capable of ruling. Her misfortune was that she was a shapely, good-looking woman whom men found extremely attractive. So although she did not want to go to bed with them, they wanted to sleep with her, and, as men tend to do, they blamed her for their own lust. Meanwhile, the chieftain Caratacus was fighting a canny guerrilla war against the Romans, using his intimate knowledge of the terrain to win many battles. But in AD 51 his troops were decisively beaten and he fled north. He arrived one morning with his battle-weary retinue at the gates of Cartimandua's court.

He begged her to shelter him, but she knew that if she did the Romans would withdraw their support from her. The Brigantes would then become a subject rather than a client nation and she would almost certainly lose her power to the men who hated her. If she faltered at this point, she would fall and plunge her people into bloody war. She had Caratacus bound hand and foot and handed him over to the Romans. This was a day when Cartimandua made many enemies. But Caratacus did not perish. He was sent back to Rome, where he made an eloquent plea for his life in the Senate, was spared and allowed to live out his days in the capital city of the Empire.

Venutius was furious at Cartimandua's betrayal of a man he saw as a hero and an ally. He organized a revolt against her. But while it was in its early stages, Cartimandua arranged for Venutius's family to be taken and hidden in a spot known only to herself and her most trusted men. She told Venutius she would kill them if he did not back down. He did so for a while, but soon teamed up with allies from outside his own immediate borders, warriors who found female rule insufferable and wanted to teach the elegant and self-possessed Cartimandua a lesson. She had no choice but to call on Roman support to help ward off these invaders.

101

> For many years Cartimandua had ruled her client kingdom in uneasy truce with her consort, Venutius. There was little love lost between the two of them, but they each had powerful supporters whom the other did not dare offend. However, eventually, in the year AD 70, nine years after Boudicca's rebellion, Cartimandua decided she had had enough of Venutius and took his armour-bearer, Vellocatus, as her consort. Of course, her enemies presumed she was driven by middle-aged lust to fancy the sturdy young warrior, but although there may well have been a sexual bond between them, Cartimandua was actually trying to build an alliance with someone she trusted and who was on her side. She had ruled for at least 30 years and now, approaching 50, she could no longer tolerate the permanent insecurity of her life.
>
> Venutius naturally revolted in protest and the Romans were brought in to protect Cartimandua once again. But this time they were not pleased with her actions. They never liked to see women take the initiative, particularly in sexual matters, and they decided to award the client ruler-ship to Venutius – with the proviso that the queen be granted honourable retirement during her remaining years.

It is interesting that, on the whole, we much prefer Boudicca. Because actually she behaves throughout her campaign as a 'man's woman' – that is, she acts in such a way that men will understand her and approve of her actions – while Cartimandua follows her own path to successful rulership. And yet they both played a vital part in the maintenance of the identity of the British nation in the first troubled years of Roman rule.

## IRISH QUEENS

Irish literature provides plenty of stories of proud and powerful queens; however, it is often not clear whether these queens had a real or a mythical existence. Did the overbearing Maeve of the *Tain* really rule Connacht? Did the Macha who gave her name to the royal seat of Emain Macha in Ulster ever live there? So far, we do not know.

Macha's stories nicely straddle the two worlds – that is, the everyday world and the Otherworld – and we can see how, as women lose power in the first world, they compensate by gaining in the second. Thus Macha, although cruelly treated by the king and his men, has the magical power to transfer her sufferings to them, to wreak the revenge of the Goddess, if you like. These queens also partake of the being of the goddess of sovereignty whose goodwill is absolutely essential for the king who is to rule the land. In the second story there may also be memories of male '*couvade*' in which, in order to gain power, men imitate the labour pains of women.

## Macha the Red-haired

tHERE were once three kings of Ulster – Dithorba, Aodh and Ciombaoth – who used to take it in turns to rule Ireland, each for seven years at a time. When Aodh died, his daughter, Macha the Red-haired, demanded to rule in his stead but was refused. Infuriated, she took up arms against the two remaining kings until they yielded to her. Then, when Dithorba died, she refused to let his five sons take his turn. She beat them in battle and married the remaining king, Ciombaoth, herself.

After the wedding she went to Connacht disguised as a leper to search out the sons of Dithorba, whom she eventually tracked down cooking a pig in the forest. She sat down and ate with them, and then persuaded each in turn to follow her deep into the wood and sleep with her. After the act, while they were weak, she tied them up and brought them back as captives to Ulster, where she set them building a fine fort which became known as Emain Macha because she used the brooch (*'eo'*) which she wore about her neck (*'muin'*) to mark out the perimeter of it.[10]

## Macha's Curse

mACHA was a woman of the Otherworld. One day she visited a widowed farmer called Crunn and, taking pity on him, decided to stay and be his wife. She cooked his food, shared his bed and brought him much good fortune. Eventually she became pregnant by him and was nearly at full term when it was time for him to attend the Assembly of the Ulstermen.

Before he went, she warned him not to mention her existence to anyone, and he promised to be careful. It so happened that at the assembly King Conchobar's horses were winning every race, and everyone was praising them up to the skies. Crunn could not resist it: 'My wife could easily beat those horses . . .' The words were out before he realized what he had said.

'Oh, really,' said the king. 'In that case we will take you into custody and send for her to prove your foolhardy boast.'

When the king's messengers arrived for Macha, she protested that she was on the point of giving birth, but they said that her husband would be killed unless she ran the race, so sadly she agreed to go with them.

Even heavily pregnant, Macha, having the gifts of the Otherworld, was amazingly fleet of foot, and she easily beat the king's horses. At the finishing line, she hunkered down and gave birth to twins. Before dying of her grotesque effort, she laid a curse on the men of Ulster, that at times of greatest need every one of them would be struck down with the same pains as she had suffered. This was henceforward called the 'debility of the men of Ulster' and the place was called 'Emain Macha', meaning 'the twins of Macha'.[11]

# QUEENS OF THE OTHERWORLD

Before we consider the stories of other 'Otherworld' queens, perhaps we should ask why, in Celtic cultures, this realm seems to be so firmly identified with the female. It may be very simply because the land is normally thought of as female; its features, such as rivers, lakes, wells and hills, are often imagined to be gateways into the other realms, into the fertile body of the Goddess. Or it could be because it is in a woman's body that the great mysteries of conception, gestation and birth occur, and therefore she is identified with 'lands of mystery' in general. Or it may be, as I have already suggested, that because women's power began to be suppressed and denigrated in the outer world, it percolated through into the 'secret insides' of the universe, where it can be contacted and tapped by men and women who know how. The story of the fairy bride is found in different forms all over Europe.

These tales, like the Welsh version that appears opposite, have a richness which spills over on to many levels. This one certainly embodies the psychological truth that the things which hurt in marriage are often the small, accidental slights which are barely noticed by the one who is guilty of them but can destroy the union over time. Juliette Wood[27] observes that marriage, involving as it does different kin groups, creates an uneasy alliance in which the wife is caught in an 'in-between' state, perhaps finding herself living among a group of people she does not know and who consider her alien. The wife can therefore be seen as a liminal character – that is, a being occupying the borderland between one world and the next.

Juliette Wood also remarks that a noticeable quality of the fairy bride in all versions of the tale is her assertiveness: she sets the conditions and acts on them. The man *must* respect the integrity of the woman; otherwise, he will lose her, and in losing her, there is a sense in which he loses his soul. This feminine assertiveness is a thread which runs through much of the Celtic material.

On an allegorical level, this tale and the story of Macha are about the relationship between the human being and the higher levels of him- or

## The Fairy of Llyn y Fan Fach

**a** YOUNG farmer was accustomed to graze his cattle on the slopes around the lake called Llyn y Fan Fach. One day he was sitting eating his lunch when he noticed a beautiful young woman floating on the surface of the lake, combing her long hair. Utterly entranced, he held out his lunchtime bread to her and said, 'Beautiful creature, will you marry me?'

The girl drifted nearer to him and reached out her hand, but she snatched it back before it touched the bread. 'Your bread is hard-baked,' she said, 'and I am not so easy to catch as you think.'

The next day he returned, this time, on the advice of his mother, with some unbaked dough, which he offered to the lake-woman when she appeared.

'Your bread is unbaked,' she said indignantly. 'I will not marry you.'

On the third day the young man brought some fresh, new bread with him, perfectly baked, and held it out once more to the lovely apparition of the lake. This time she stepped out of the water, sniffed the bread and smiled, took his hand and agreed to marry him. She warned him, however, that she was not an ordinary human woman and that if, in the course of their life together, he struck her three times, then their marriage would be over and she would have to return to the lake.

The two married and were very happy. The man was never even tempted to raise his hand to his wife. She bore him three healthy sons, his farm prospered, the cows yielded plenty of milk and it seemed they were living the perfect life. Then one day she forgot to mend his shirt and jestingly he tapped her on the shoulder to remind her. She turned to him with a grave face and reminded him of the taboo on him hitting her. He laughed it off and promised never to forget again. But a couple of years later, while slightly the worse for drink, he slapped her on the back in congratulations for a joke well told. This time she shook her head sadly and quietly left the room. The third occasion was a gentle tap on the cheek. He could scarcely believe it when his wife rose up and left the house saying, 'The last blow is struck. The marriage contract is broken.'

The man was too heartbroken ever to go back to the shores of the lake into which his fairy wife had returned, but her sons often did, gazing into its depths and calling out to the mother who had abandoned them while they were still growing up.

Finally, one day she heard their pleas and appeared to them, carrying a leather bag in her hand which she gave to the eldest boy, saying, 'Your mission in life will be to heal the sick. In this bag are the healing secrets of the Otherworld.'

She took the three of them and showed them all the different herbs of the mountainside and told them for which ailment each could be used.

> Then she walked out into the lake and disappeared into its waters
> without a backward look.
>
> Her three sons became the famous physicians of Myddfai who were
> appointed court doctors to the Prince of South Wales. Their descendants
> continued to practise healing right down to the end of the nineteenth
> century.[26]

herself which we sometimes call the soul. You cannot apply the
common-sense rules of every day to matters concerning the soul. For
example, you may say, 'Surely it doesn't matter if I don't pay my tube fare.
After all, I know there's no one on duty at the station at this time of
night', but the act of fare-dodging may injure the soul, which is a much
more delicate organism than the ego, and if bruised and battered too much
by such acts of dishonesty, it may slip away and leave us bereft of our
contact with the higher self, just as the fairy slips back into the element
whence she came.

## Scottish Fairy Queens

However, the supernatural woman, the fairy queen, can be a much more
ambiguous figure too, as we see in the Scottish tales of Thomas Rhymer and
Tam Lin, now best known as revived folk ballads. Thomas meets a 'lady that
was brisk and bold' and takes her at first for the Queen of Heaven. She
quickly sets him right: she is the 'Queen of Elfland', which seems to be an
intermediate place between heaven and hell. Thomas goes with her there for
seven years and learns the secret of telling the future, which is why he is
called 'true Thomas'. He comes back to the ordinary world and becomes
famous as a prophet, but one day the queen sends a hart and a hind to guide
him back to her and he ups and leaves this world without a second thought.

The ballad of Tam Lin tells of a young man kept in thrall by the fairy
queen whose true love, Janet, rescues him from her and her hellish realm.
Tam Lin tells Janet:

> And pleasant is the fairy land,
> But an eerie tale to tell,
> Ay at the end of seven years
> We pay a tiend* to hell;
> I am sae fair and fu o flesh,
> I feard it be mysel.

---

\* forfeit

Now, if we ask ourselves once again why the Otherworld is connected with women, we have a clue to help us to yet another answer. This is what will happen when Tam is being saved from his awful fate of becoming a sacrifice to hell:

> They'll turn me in your arms, lady,
> Into an esk and adder;
> But hold me fast and fear me not,
> I am your bairn's father.
>
> They'll turn me into a bear sae grim;
> And then a lion bold;
> But hold me fast, and fear me not,
> As ye shall love your child.
>
> Again they'll turn me in your arms
> To a red hot gaud* of airn;
> But hold me fast, and fear me not,
> I'll do to you nae harm.
>
> At last they'll turn me in your arms
> Into the burning gleed;†
> Then throw me into well water,
> O throw me in wi speed.
>
> And then I'll be your ain true love,
> I'll turn into a naked knight;
> Then cover me wi your green mantle
> And cover me out o sight.[28]

It sounds very much as if Tam is coming out of a shamanic trance, changing himself back through various totem animals and objects into his own human shape. This is something he has learned in the realm of the fairy queen – that is, the female shaman. Janet can save him because she, like her fairy adversary, is at home in the Otherworld. Through the experience of giving birth, women visit the furthest shores of existence, where the gates of life and death stand open. This was particularly true before modern medicine made birth a much safer experience; in ancient times women often died of it. Even nowadays birth is a painful, convulsive and miraculous event which the ego cannot control: the body and the psyche run it, leaving out the ego. It seems to belong to another order of reality and there is no easily available equivalent for men. This may be why so many men feel the need to risk

---

* bar
† coal

their lives in dangerous pursuits or in war – or in Tam Lin's case, by training as a shaman!

His true love, Janet, is saving him for the Christian Church from the clutches of this pagan practice. It must have continued well into Christian times, because there are so many Scottish border ballads and tales about young men being whisked off by fairy women. They were also of course called witches.

## Breton Fairy Queens

The Breton tales come from a later period and have more of the usual European fairytale flavour about them, but in those recorded by F. M. Luzel in the mid-nineteenth century there are many pre-Christian traces, one of the commonest being the figure of the wise magical woman who guides the young hero to freedom and/or a happy marriage with the right princess. In many of the tales the princess herself, with her sun-coloured hair, is both the goal and the guide. The following story is based on a version collected by Luzel.[29]

### The Princess of the Shining Star

ONCE in a snowy December a young miller was out duck-shooting. He took aim at a fine duck splashing in the pond and fired, but as soon as the bullet hit the bird, it changed into a beautiful princess. She thanked him warmly for returning her to human form. Three demons had imprisoned her in the form of a duck and now she asked the young man to help her escape entirely from their clutches.

'You will need to spend three nights in succession in the old ruined manor house where 12 devils will torment you. But whatever they do to you, do not worry, because I have a special ointment which will restore you to health. Then the three casks of gold and silver which lie buried under the hearthstone of the manor will be yours. As I will be, if you so desire.'

'Even if there were 100 devils instead of 12, I would do it,' said the miller.

That night he lit a fire in the hearth of the old manor and waited for the devils. They were delighted to find him there and threw him from one end of the hall to the other with ruthless abandon, as if he were a ball. All the way through his ordeal the miller did not speak a word, because the princess had told him he must be silent. The devils finally tossed him out of the window into the snow and left him for dead.

*The Queen of Elfland, initiator of men.*

109

The next morning the princess brought him back to life with her ointment. The next night he faced the devils again.

'I smell a Christian,' said the wickedest devil of all, and popped the miller into a cauldron and boiled him up.

By the time the cock crowed in the morning, his flesh was falling off the bone. But the princess found him and restored him with her ointment once again.

On the third night the devils held a debate to decide what particularly horrible torture they could inflict on the poor miller to finish him off. Eventually they decided to roast and eat him, but just as they were going to skewer him and lay him on the fire, the cock crowed and the princess arrived to save him.

They embraced in great joy and relief, and the princess uncovered the treasure hidden under the hearthstone and gave it all to the miller.

'As for me,' she said regretfully, 'I have to undertake a journey which will last a year and a day. After that we will be together for ever.'

The miller was sorry to see her go, but he consoled himself by taking a long holiday with his friend, to visit far-off lands. But after eight months they came back, so anxious was the miller not to miss his rendezvous with the princess.

On the way home they met an old woman selling apples. The miller's friend urged him not to buy any, but the miller bought three.

The next day, while waiting for the princess at the spot they had appointed in the wood, he ate one of the apples and fell asleep. When she arrived in her beautiful star-coloured carriage, she was very sad and told the friend, who was waiting too, that the old woman who sold the apples had obviously been a witch. She gave the friend a golden pear and a handkerchief for her lover and urged him to make sure he stayed awake the next day.

But when she returned, in a moon-coloured chariot this time, the miller had absent-mindedly eaten another of the apples and was asleep again. She handed over another pear and another handkerchief and went on her way.

The day after, when she came in a sun-coloured coach, the same thing happened yet again. The princess was very sad indeed and told the friend that now the only way the miller could find her would be to come to the Kingdom of the Shining Star. He would have to cross three powers and three seas to get there, which he could do only with great trouble and pain. She left a third pear and a third handkerchief for him, before wrenching herself away.

When the miller awoke he was desolate, but vowed he would reach the Kingdom of the Shining Star no matter how hard the journey might be. He set out straight away, taking with him the golden pears and the handkerchiefs which the princess had left for him, and after walking without stopping for days and nights, he entered a great forest in which he wandered aimlessly for a long time. Finally, he spotted a light in the distance and, stumbling up to it, found himself in a hut inhabited by an old gentleman with a long white beard. The old man welcomed him warmly, saying he had not had human company for 1,800 years, and made him a present of a pair of enchanted gaiters which would allow him to cover seven leagues with each step he took.

The next morning he made great progress with the gaiters, flying along above the countryside over rivers, mountains and forests. At sunset he found another hut like the old man's and in it found an old woman who tried to get rid of him as quickly as she could.

'Young man, run for your life,' she said. 'My sons, the giants January, February and March, will eat you up as soon as look at you.'

But it was too late. The giants were already on their way home. 'I will just have to pretend you are my nephew,' said the old woman. It was a close thing. The giants very nearly ate the miller for their dinner, but in the end they became friends instead and the next morning February took him on his back and carried him across three seas to the Kingdom of the Shining Star. Then March took over and helped him over the wall of the city. At last he was there.

The landlady at the inn where he stayed told him that the Princess of the Shining Star was getting married that day to a prince she did not like, and that the wedding procession would be passing the inn. The miller laid a gold pear and a handkerchief out on a table in front of the inn and waited. As the princess passed on her way to the church, she spotted them and the miller and suddenly pretended to be indisposed, so that the wedding was put off until the next day. The next day the same thing happened, but on the third day she could contain herself no longer. The princess and the miller fell into each other's arms.

The princess did not marry the prince but ran away with the young miller to Gueodet in Lower Brittany, where they were married in church. Never was such feasting and rejoicing seen – except maybe in a dream.

Buried in this delightful and complex tale is the idea of the sacred marriage only attained at the end of a long difficult quest. The marriage symbolizes the union of male *self* with female *soul* which marks the completion of the individual's journey towards enlightenment and wholeness. The princess-soul can guide the young man, but she cannot do it for him, and although he wants her very badly, he cannot stop himself falling asleep. To *fall asleep* is to give up on the continuous and unremitting effort necessary to progress through the different levels of consciousness which finally lead us to the truth. This is a motif which crops up again in the next narrative.

# ISLANDS OF WOMEN

In medieval Celtic times the bards and monks write of 'islands of women' which float in the western sea, paradisaical places where there is delicious food, drink, sweet music, love . . . everything that the heart desires. This might sound like a rather material kind of spirituality, but in the extremely beautiful eighth-century poem 'The Voyage of Bran' the woman who leads Bran on a voyage of mystical enlightenment represents the fairy queen in her highest form, a being who may slip between the worlds and guide others who wish to do so. In her hand she holds a 'branch of silver with white blossoms', symbol of the Otherworld, which she gives to Bran. In the song she sings him, she tries to persuade him to begin the journey which leads to truth, warning him not to fall asleep:

> Do not fall on a bed of sloth,
> Let not thy intoxication overcome thee;
> Begin a voyage across the clear sea,
> If perchance thou mayst reach the land of women.

She sings a prophecy of the birth of Christ:

> A great birth will come after ages,
> That will not be in a lofty place,
> The son of a woman whose mate will not be known,
> He will seize the rule of the many thousands.

The woman departs and Bran sets out on his journey. He meets the sea god Manannan, who sings of the magical son he is going to sire:

> He will delight the company of every fairy knoll
> He will be the darling of every goodly land,
> He will make known secrets – a course in wisdom –
> In the world, without being feared.
> He will be in the shape of every beast,
> Both on azure sea and on land,
> He will be a dragon before hosts at the onset,
> He will be a wolf of every great forest.[1]

Prophecies of the coming of Christ combine with prophecies of the birth of a magical hero-child without any sense of contradiction. The poem joins together almost seamlessly the pagan yearning for sensual enjoyment and ecstasy with the new Christian ideals of redemption and transcendence. There is no sense of conflict or strain; on the contrary, there are intimations of a tradition of knowledge and wisdom which transcends the labels 'pagan' or 'Christian' of which, it seems, women are the guardians. Bran then travels

112

on to the Land of Women. The chief woman welcomes him and throws him a ball of thread, which sticks to his palm. Using this, she pulls their coracle into the harbour. On the island they find 'thrice nine beds', a bed for every couple and plenty of wonderful food. It seems to the men that they are there for a year, though in fact it is many years. When homesickness seizes one of their number, Nechtan, he persuades the others to make the return trip home, but the woman warns that none of them should ever touch the land. When they sail back to Ireland and reach land, Nechtan leaps out of the boat on to the shore and turns instantly to ashes. Hundreds of years have passed while Bran and his men have been voyaging for what seemed just a few years.

The poem is clearly a mystical allegory to which we have lost some of the keys. One intriguing question for us is whether the Land of Women was purely symbolic. Given that we know there were islands of women priestesses off the coast of Gaul, it seems reasonable to suppose that this one might be based on a real place or places. A place with a harbour so difficult to navigate that sailors had to be guided in by a rope; where they were sexually initiated by the priestesses; where the sense of time was different; and which changed them so completely that they could never land on their native shores again, never be their 'old selves'. It sounds like a mystery school on the model of the ancient Greek ones found at Samothrace or Samos or Symi, only run entirely by women teachers.

The above is pure speculation, but if it has any truth in it, how frustrating that we have no better record of such places, and how unfortunate that the spirit of reconciliation and peace which pervades this poem could not stop Christianity taking the patriarchal Roman direction in which the guardian or priestess role for women was diminished almost to invisibility.

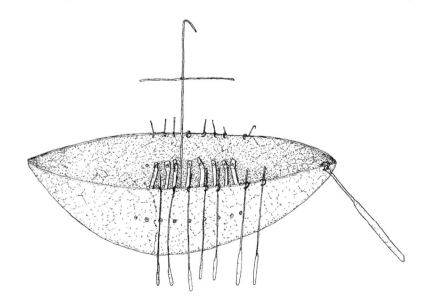

*Voyages to the 'islands of women'. Golden boat from Broighter, County Derry, first century BC.* (Craig Chapman)

113

# 7 WARRIORS, WITCHES AND WISE WOMEN

## THE POWER OF THE DARK

The dark side of the Celtic woman is perhaps the most fascinating because it challenges our idealized notions of how female power should express itself. In the old narratives this kind of woman is either portrayed with fear and delighted disapproval as in the myriad tales of weird women and witches like Morgan le Fay, or with profound respect, as in the story of Scathach, 'the best teacher of warriors in the world'. In both categories we have characters who draw on the archetype of woman as destroyer and tester, as much a part of the female psyche as the mother or nurturer, but much more uncomfortable to contemplate!

### Scathach, the Shadowy One

CUCHULAIN caught his breath and glared at the bridge which led to Scathach's castle. It was a fiendish contraption: low at both ends and high in the middle, designed so that as soon as someone stepped on one end, the other end flew up like a see-saw and threw him on his back. Three times already Cuchulain had landed on his back. He didn't mind the bruises, but the jeering and hooting from the crowd of men watching were more than he could stand.

He had to gain entry. Scathach was the best teacher of warriors in the western world, and he wanted to be the best warrior in the western world, not just in Ireland. He was a natural fighter, strong and brave and skilful, but he knew those skills needed honing and refining. He also knew Scathach was the only one who could do it. He had made a long arduous journey to this island on the wild coast of Alba. He was not ready to be sent away.

He filled his lungs with air and panted fast so that he went into his battle-trance. Then he launched himself into his famous salmon-leap and landed in the middle of the bridge. Before the far end had time to fly up at him, he had bounded safely over it on to solid ground. He finished by thrusting his spear at the gate so that it fell flat before him, and in he walked.

When Scathach heard about this, she said, 'Hmm – this sounds like someone who's already had a thorough training!'

She sent her daughter Uathach out to meet the young warrior and Uathach returned completely overwhelmed by his radiant good looks and lithe, well-muscled body.

'You like him don't you?' said Scathach.

'I do indeed.'

'Then sleep with him, if that's what you want.'

'I wouldn't have to force myself, so long as it's what he wants too.'

Uathach played a game with Cuchulain. She pretended to be a servant, bringing him food and drink, and flirting with him along the way. Eventually he grabbed her and in their amorous rough-and-tumble accidentally bent her finger back so that she cried out. One of Scathach's soldiers, Cochar Cruibne, rushed to her aid, thinking that she was being attacked. He used all his best tricks to tackle Cuchulain, but the younger man felled him and cut off his head.

Scathach was appalled. Cochar had been one of her best men and a loyal friend, but Cuchulain had not known that and killed him thinking he was an intruder. The young warrior assured her that he would take the dead man's place, lead her army and be her champion too.

The next three days Cuchulain spent with Uathach, learning the arts of love. Then she told him that if he wanted to learn the arts of *war* as well, he needed to take decisive action. He must go to the big yew tree in which Scathach rested during training sessions, leap up into its branches and threaten her with his sword, pointing it right between her breasts. He should not release her until she had promised him three things.

Cuchulain performed the act exactly as demanded and Scathach promised to grant him three wishes, the deepest desires of his heart, if he could say them all within one breath. He demanded that she should give him the best training possible in the advanced arts of war, grant him a dowry for his marriage and tell him what his future would hold. Scathach consented to do those three things.

At this time Scathach was engaged in a local war with her neighbour Aife, known as the hardest woman warrior in the world. On the day of battle she gave Cuchulain a sleeping draught because she did not want him hurt in this petty skirmish. The draught would have lasted 24 hours on anyone else, but on Cuchulain it lasted only an hour. He leapt up and joined Scathach's two sons in battle against Aife and her best men. Cuchulain had killed several of Aife's men before she stopped the battle and challenged Scathach to single combat. As Scathach's champion, Cuchulain volunteered to fight, but first he took his teacher aside and asked her what Aife loved most in the world.

'No doubt about that,' said Scathach, 'her horses, her chariot and her charioteer.'

When Cuchulain met Aife in combat, it was not long before she had smashed his sword down to the grip.

'Oh, look,' he cried out, 'your chariot and horses have tumbled into the valley. They will all be killed!'

As Aife turned away in the direction of the valley, Cuchulain grabbed her by the breasts, slung her over his shoulder and carried her back behind his lines. Then he threw her on the ground and pointed a sword to her throat.

'A life for a life!' Aife choked.

'If you grant me three desires.'

'Ask them in one breath and they are yours.'

'Give me hostages for Scathach, promising never to attack her again, your company tonight at your fort and, lastly, agree to bear me a son.'

Aife must have thought this a small price for her life, and that night she slept with Cuchulain, and was able to tell him soon after that she had conceived and that the child would be a boy. The young warrior left his son a ring and asked that he should come to Ireland when he was big enough for the ring to fit. He was to be called Connla and was to tell no man his name, yield to no man and refuse no man combat.

Back in Scathach's camp, Cuchulain's training in the magical arts of war continued. By the time the great teacher had finished with him, he could juggle nine apples all at one time; he could jump on a lance in flight and straighten up erect on its point; he could drive a sickle-chariot and truss up a warrior on the points of spears. He could manage all sorts of tricks of sound and breath, such as the snapping mouth and the hero's scream, both designed to cast desolation into the heart of the enemy. He had perfected the famous salmon-leap, the spurt of speed, and could throw the hideous gae-bolga, a javelin which opened into thirty barbs as it entered a man's flesh.

When it was time for him to return to his own country Scathach prepared herself to enter a prophetic trance and tell him the secrets of his destiny. She held up her two hands, made a tunnel of them and, looking through it with the Light of Foresight shining into her eyes, she chanted. She told Cuchulain she saw blood and slaughter and victory lying ahead of him, a life full of triumph and women's love which would end when he was 33 years old.

'A short life it will be, Cuchulain,' she said, 'but a glorious one. I salute you.'

Scathach's story comes from the narrative *Tochmarc Emire*, written down in the tenth or eleventh century, which means its origins may be much much older.[30] Scathach emerges from it as a shrewd, tough woman of few words, probably in early middle age (she has a grown-up daughter and two warrior sons), with the knowledge and ability to teach the most refined and

Below: *Spearhead from the River Thames. Celtic warriors also wielded invisible weapons.* (British Museum)

Opposite: *Scathach, the teacher of warriors, with Uathach and Aife.*

117

curious forms of martial arts. Some of the feats described are clearly physical impossibilities, which raises the question of whether what she was teaching was not only technical skill with arms but also the magical art of creating illusions, or, in modern jargon, ways of 'psyching out' the enemy. The way that Cuchulain beats Aife, who seems to be his superior as a sword-wielder, by directing her attention away from himself while he grabs her, suggests this may well be the case. The basic art of stage-magic is the ability to direct attention at will. If you can persuade a magician to show you one of his routines over and over again, you may eventually be able to spot how he does it – for example, by making your eyes follow the action of one hand while he performs his trick with the other.

Everything that happens to Cuchulain on the island (yes, it's another island of women) seems to be part of a ritualized system of training. It could even be that his spending three days with Uathach, Scathach's daughter, is part of this. She may have been assigned to teach him about the nature of sexual energy and how to transform it into other forms of power. Certainly, right from the beginning she and her mother treat him not as a prospective husband and son-in-law but as a young man of extraordinary abilities who needs to learn to focus and channel his force properly if he is not to squander it in dangerous and destructive behaviour, such as the killing of poor Cochar.

The way in which he has to *force* Scathach to teach him and *force* Aife to bear him a son makes both activities sound like ritual initiations. There are many traditions in which the aspirant has to perform an unusual act to persuade a teacher to take him on. Given that this is a warrior tradition, it is not surprising that the act in this case is to *take* power and control rather than be offered it. It is possible that the battle with Aife was in fact a put-up job, designed as a test for the young warrior, to see what he would do when his physical skills were not adequate to the situation. We can then ask ourselves if this is just a fascinating tale or if such places as Scathach's island, where groups of wise women initiated young men into the arts of love and war, really did exist.

Scathach's castle is traditionally located on the island of Skye, and there is, near Tarskavaig, a ruined castle from the medieval period called Dun Scaich or Dun Scaith which is associated with legends of Scathach and Cuchulain. It is said to have been surrounded in the olden days by seven ramparts, crowned by iron palisades and protected by a pit full of snakes and beaked toads. It is built upon a rock with precipitous sides and approached by a causeway which leads to a bridge over a gully in the rock – which sounds as if it could once have been the treacherous 'Pupil's Bridge'. There is a boulder nearby called Cuchulain's Rock to which, it is said, the hero used to tie his hound, Luath.

In later medieval times the castle belonged to the Macdonalds of Sleat, so it is interesting that the legend of Scathach persists so strongly, albeit sometimes with the somewhat distorted slant that Cuchulain was in love with Scathach, who was an accomplished musician on a three-stringed harp which could be used to make people laugh or cry or fall asleep!

The name 'Scathach' means 'Shadowy One' and is a Celticized form of 'Skadi', the Viking goddess after whom Scandinavia is named. In more primitive times, Skadi apparently had to be propitiated by the spilling of male blood in a sacrificial rite which involved the cutting off of the genitals.[21]

We know that the Vikings were in Skye from AD 798 onwards, so if there had been here at one time a cult centre for the worship of this goddess, then no wonder Cuchulain had to conquer her quickly before she turned him into her yearly victim. Certainly, the Vikings had strong traditions of women warriors, and it could be that Scathach was a Scandinavian woman who would impart her martial secrets to Celtic warriors for a price. Robert Graves even suggests that Scotland is named after Scathach/Skadi, 'Scotia' being a later version of her name.[31] The western islands of Scotland are particularly rich in legends about strong-minded, dangerous women. It is said that a warrior queen and her female soldiers murdered St Donaan of Eigg by locking him and his worshippers into a church and setting fire to it. However, later that night a mysterious, unearthly light led the queen and her warriors into a loch where they were all drowned. The loch is now called the Loch of the Big Women — which could be a memory of the sturdy, well-muscled warrior-witches of the Dark Ages like Scathach and Aife.[32]

In St Kilda to this day there is a complex beehive house known as the Amazon's House. It was referred to by a visitor there in 1697 as 'the House of the Female Warrior'. She was reputed to have been a princess from Harris in the Outer Hebrides.[33]

# THE MORRIGAN

With the Morrigan, who is usually presented as the Irish war goddess, we come close to the archetype which lies behind the wicked witch of the children's storybooks. Her name means 'great queen' or 'phantom queen', but there is also an association with the sea (*mor*) which becomes stronger in the later form of the name, 'Morgan'. This reference also appears in 'Ar-*mor*-ica', the old name for Brittany.

The Morrigan, with or without her two sisters, Badb and Macha (they come under various other names too), haunts battlefields in the form of a crow, picking at the entrails of the slaughtered men, shrieking in delight as she hops across the tips of spears and swords, relishing the battle chaos and the carnage. Sometimes she takes sides and helps her favoured ones to victory. Sometimes, in her role as the 'washer at the ford', she is seen

## The Morrigan Meets Cuchulain

**t**HE MORRIGAN tells Cuchulain she is King Buan's daughter and offers him her treasure and her love. Cuchulain tersely replies that it was not for 'a woman's backside' that he took on this war. The Morrigan then threatens to hinder him, to appear in battle as an eel, a she-wolf and a hornless red cow. He swears he will wound her in whatever form she takes. Sure enough, at a low point in Cuchulain's battle fortunes, she appears and tries to bring him down. He wounds her as he has promised. Then later, in her 'old-lady' form once more, she appears before the battle-weary Cuchulain, milking a cow with three teats. She gives him a drink of milk and he blesses her, thus healing the wounds he has inflicted on her before.

'You said you would never heal me,' said the Morrigan.

'I wouldn't have done it if I'd known it was you,' said Cuchulain.

laundering bloody linen in the stream and becomes an ill omen prophesying death in battle. (The banshee, whose shrieking is believed to herald death in the family, is related to this aspect of the goddess.) She is usually depicted as old, ugly and vicious, although she seems to be able to take any shape she wants, as when she encounters Cuchulain in the *Tain* (above).

What is going on in this battle-within-a-battle between the young hero, dealer of death, and the old goddess, bringer of death? At one level it is the usual male–female conflict, the dance of difference: 'Don't distract me while I'm making war', 'If you reject me I'll find ways of hurting you', 'I'll hurt you back', 'But you love me really, don't you? Look, you've kissed me better!'

At another level we have the defiance of the beautiful, strong, skilful male who can vanquish and control almost everything in the universe – except his own death. Death will come to him, the great warrior, just as it does to the meanest female slave. And that fact is hard to swallow, particularly hard because death comes in female form as the Morrigan.

Death in battle in Iron or Dark Age Ireland must have often been a brutal and agonizing business – limbs hacked off, gaping rips and wounds, infections and gangrene, disfiguring mutilations of the face and body, terrible pain with nothing but alcohol to deaden it. The process of dying was truly terrible, although actual death presumably came as a welcome release.

The battle between Cuchulain and the Morrigan is also the battle between life and death, in which neither can finally win because the balance must always be maintained. The Morrigan is the goddess of the reality of death and its necessity, hated and feared by the young but accepted by the old and the wise.

*The Morrigan meets Cuchulain.*

# THE DEATH GODDESS IN OTHER FORMS

Among the Cimbri, a Germanic (or possibly Celtic) tribe, priestesses of the death goddess would perform the ceremonial of cutting the throats of prisoners and catching their blood in a bowl. As already mentioned, the enormous krater found in the grave of a Celtic woman at Vix may have been used to hold the blood of sacrifice. Among the Rus people (emigrated Vikings), it was a priestess who would kill the slave girl who had chosen to accompany her master to the grave. Thus women who give birth in blood were deemed to be at home in the blood-lettings which bring death too. It is easy to see how the Morrigan and the other goddesses associated with death, like Andraste, were considered sinister and fearful, but we should remember that they are performing a function that is necessary for the continuation of life – dissolving old forms, breaking them down to their component parts, so that new forms and beings may be created. On an individual level, if we prepare for death, we may well be able to lead a better life.

*Helen Mirren as Morgan le Fay, with Nicole Williamson as Merlin in the film* Excalibur. (John Matthews)

In Ireland, until quite recently, special women would be called in to 'keen' for the dead at a funeral or wake, their uninhibited howling and wailing providing an expression for the grief of the friends and family of the deceased. In the Highlands of Scotland too, up until the nineteenth century, there were mourning women who would follow the body to the burial ground, striking and drumming on the coffin from time to time and reciting the genealogy of the family to remind the mourners of the continuity of life. What the mourning women would say about the dead was not always good: Carmichael quotes an occasion on Tiree when the woman employed to do the job took the opportunity to tell some home truths about the wicked man she was burying:

> Thou art gone, thou art gone!
> Thou art gone and hast remained not!
> We shall see thee no more,
> Black Evil Donald![11]

We see the male–female, life–death battle arise again centuries later in the Arthurian legends, in which the Morrigan has become Morgan and is portrayed as the good Arthur's wicked half-sister who tricks him into sleeping with her. The offspring of this union is Mordred, the 'mother's son' who eventually kills his noble father. Morgan le Fay is the first in a long line of wicked underworld women (remember her underground magic-chamber in the film *Excalibur*?), the kind of characters like Cruella de Ville in *One Hundred and One Dalmatians* whom children love to hate. But they are genuinely terrifying because of the connection with the death goddess, the Kali or Cailleach of our Celtic past.

*Kali, the Hindu goddess of destruction. Does the name 'Caledonia' come from her?*
(Craig Chapman)

123

*The Beare Peninsula, home of the Hag of Beare.*
(Michael J. Stead)

# THE BRETON MORGANS

In Brittany the name 'Morgan' has a different flavour. The Morgans seem here to be sea fairies or sea goddesses. In one tale, quoted by Evans Wentz, the Morgan is presented as a siren figure whose beautiful song draws men to her. But before they can reach her, their boats flounder on the rocks, so that she embraces only corpses. This sort of tale clearly has connection with other European legends of Rhine Maidens and sirens who lure men to their doom.

## *The Drowning of the City of Is*

DAHUT was the daughter of Gradlon, King of Is, a city state on the sea-coast of Brittany. One day while walking on the beach, she met a tall, sombre-suited young man with dark, depthless eyes – the 'black prince' they called him. She fell in love with him and she used to creep away from her father's castle to be with him at night, to dance, feast and carouse with his decadent friends. One night he asked her to prove her love for him by stealing the key to the floodgates in the sea-dyke which protected the city. This key was worn by her father on a chain around his neck at all times, so only she had the chance to get it.

She was so utterly under the spell of the black prince that she approached her father one night and playfully asked to borrow the key. Her father gave it to her and she handed it over to her lover. He used it to open the floodgates, so that soon water began to trickle through the streets of Is.

St Guenolé was up early saying his prayers when he felt water seeping through the wool of his robes as he knelt on the stone floor. He soon realized what had happened and ran to the king, shouting, 'Great king, arise! The floodgates are open and the sea is no longer restrained!'

The old king roused himself, mounted his horse and set out with Guenolé to escape, but as they waded through the rising waters on their horses he spotted his daughter clinging to a doorway, just about to be swept away. He took her up behind him and tried to make headway against the waves, but it was no good – the waters were gaining on them all the time.

'Throw that demon you have behind you to the waves and we will be saved!' shouted St Guenolé.

Gradlon flung his daughter down into the abyss and with that the waters drew back for a moment, so that he and Guenolé could escape.

Since that time the fishermen say that on certain clear, moonlit nights they have seen Dahut sitting on the rocks, where the old city of Is once was, combing her hair and singing. Today she is known under the name of Mari-Morgan, the daughter who sings amid the sea.

Dahut's awakening sexuality 'opens the floodgates' and causes the drowning of a civilization ruled by her father.[34] She also perishes, but is reborn as a classic sea siren.

Even though this Morgan is neither war goddess nor witch, but simply a girl who falls in love with the devil and loses her head, she is still clearly the bringer of death, seen in the tale in opposition to the Christian St Guenolé, who is portrayed as the bringer of life and redemption.

# THE CAILLEACH BHEARA – THE HAG OF BEARE

The word *'cailleach'* simply means old woman. Stories about her are still told in Ireland and Scotland, with many regional variations, but she seems to come originally from the Beare peninsula in west Cork, in the old province of Munster, which Alwyn and Brinsley Rees have suggested was always associated with women, the Otherworld and the dead.[35] At the tip of the peninsula is an island which is regarded as her residence, 'Inis Boi', *'boi'* being a word for 'cow'. Perhaps originally a fertility priestess lived there.

We meet her in person in the extraordinary ninth-century poem 'The Hag of Beare', where she introduces herself as a miserable old, yellow-skinned woman lamenting her lost youth. Then she was beautiful, drank wine and consorted with kings. Now her only choice seems to be to take the veil, though she does not seem to be very pious by nature.

In her goddess form, it was said that she has 'passed into seven periods of youth, so that every husband used to pass to death from her of old age, so that her grandchildren and great-grandchildren were peoples and races'. We have a sense here of that continuity which runs through the line of women way back into time, and which men cannot feel, being born, as they are, from a body which is unlike their own. But in the poem the Cailleach seems to have lost her power of regeneration with the coming of Christianity, in which there is no role for the powerful, magical older woman unless she wants to abnegate her sexuality into nunhood: 'My right eye has been taken from me to be sold for a land that will be for ever mine, the left eye has been taken also, to make my claim to that land more secure.'

Rosalind Clarke, in *The Great Queens*, suggests that this blindness is a result of the old age which came upon her when she renounced her pagan immortality for Christianity.[14]

In Ireland the Cailleach is associated with stories embodying various kinds of natural wisdom, to do with corn and harvesting, health and fertility. In Scotland she is seen more as the 'storm hag', bringer of bad weather. Her other names there include Beire, Gyre-Carline, Mag Moullach and Gentle Annie – this last ironical. Marian McNeill says she is the one-eyed goddess of winter, enemy of growth, whose chief seat is Ben Nevis

127

and who ushers in winter by washing her plaid in the whirlpool of Corryvreckan. 'Before the washing, it is said, the roar of a coming tempest is heard by people on the coast for a distance of 20 miles, for a period of three days until the cauldron boils. When the washing is over, the plaid of old Scotland is virgin white.'[6]

Barbara Walker[21] claims that the old name for Scotland, Caledonia, comes from Cailleach and that it is also related to Kali, the Hindu destroyer goddess. Since the Celts and the Indians share a common Indo-European heritage, this is possible, but perhaps a little far-fetched.

Opposite: *The Cailleach, one-eyed winter goddess.*

Below: *Once the Cailleach has washed her clothes 'the plaid of old Scotland is virgin white'.*
(Michael J. Stead)

# WITCHES

Connections have been traced between the magical traditions of the Celts and the practices of witches much later in European history, although some scholars argue that witchcraft is a survival from the older pre-Celtic races. Our natural horror at the way witches, mainly women, were tortured and killed in the witch-hunts of the 1600s makes it hard to disentangle what these women actually did. All the more so since their torturers often put words into their mouths, so that the 'evidence' obtained was merely a reflection of their depraved expectations.

However, some women confessed without torture and it may be that their testimony reflects a secret tradition which did exist, hidden for the most part from the eagle eye of the church. One of these was Isabel Gowdie, a young Scottish woman who gave an account of her activities before the Sheriff of Auldern, Nairn, in 1662, claiming that she and her companions could fly on straws, transform themselves into cats, hares and jackdaws, and visit and talk to the fairy queen. There were sexual orgies in which Isabel had intercourse with the devil, whom she described as a 'meikle black man'.[32]

The sexual details in Isabel's and others' confessions suggest that the deep understanding of polarity and the power it can build had not been completely lost in Christian times but had surfaced, usually in corrupt and distorted form, in the witch covens. One can understand how lively, power-seeking women, denied an outlet in the Church, might turn to witchcraft, and one can also understand how they would sometimes succumb to the temptation to use the power obtained in the wrong way.

If you think the stories of evil spells and black magic worked on neighbours' cows are a far-fetched male fabrication, ask around your women friends. I have two friends, one powerful in a worldly sphere, the other with sincere spiritual interests, who both confess to making effigy dolls in girlhood and sticking pins into them. In both cases they got a salutary shock when the revenge ritual seemed to work. Needless to say, neither of them has ever tried black magic since, but it does prove the appeal of such things to the undeveloped female psyche.

We know there were also 'white witches', wise women who practised a benevolent form of earth magic, including healing using the properties of herbs, minerals and crystals. They were often midwives too, possessors of knowledge about the female mysteries of conception, menarche and menopause, as well as birth.

Some of these white witches also had a profound understanding of weather which would enable them to predict the best times for sowing and harvesting. They also appear to control the weather, an attribute which comes up in several Highland tales. Or maybe they really *could* control the weather.

## The Barraman and the Two Witches

ONALD was a fisherman from the Isle of Barra in the west of Scotland and he had a neighbour called Mary, who had a cow but no croft to graze it on. One day, just before Donald was to set out on a trip to Glasgow, she asked him if she might graze her cow on his croft, just until he returned from his travels. He saw no reason to say no.

Donald's boat made good time on the way to Glasgow and, once they had unloaded their cargo of fish and oil, the crew bought plenty of supplies for themselves – hemp, hooks, tobacco, sugar, tea, things like that. Then they loaded up the boat and set off back home. A stiff wind helped them on their way right up until they got to the sound of Mull, and Donald was feeling happy and satisfied at his successful trip. They fetched a jar of whisky to have a little drink to celebrate their imminent return home.

But as they set out to cross the Minch to Barra the wind suddenly dropped, and while they were scratching their heads about this, a gale blew up from west-northwest and they had no choice but to turn round and put into the harbour at the north end of Coll. They spent the night there and set out again in the morning. But when they reached the same spot the wind started up again. They battled against it for a while but eventually they had to give up and go back to Coll.

This business of the wind which stopped them crossing the sound went on and on past harvest time, and then past potato-lifting time. The nights drew in and still they could not get home. They sat down one night in the house where they were lodging and began to tell stories to pass the time. The crofter's horse came home covered with hailstones, and had to be dried off and comforted.

Donald was sitting close to the old lady of the house, and he heard her whisper, 'Oh, poor old horse, isn't that cailleach from Barra playing havoc with the weather tonight, so that you have to take shelter under the roof to escape from it?'

'Mistress,' he said, 'could I have a word with you later?'

'Indeed you can, Donald. When the others go to bed, we will stay up and have a wee talk.'

Mistress MacLean confirmed his suspicions: the woman whose cow was grazing on his croft was keeping them wind-bound so she would not have to give up the favour.

'But I will give you a remedy,' said the old lady. 'I will get my cuigeal* and spin a fathom of thread and I will put one knot, then another, then a third on it, and if you follow my instructions carefully you will be at home on Barra by the morning.'

* distaff

So Donald and his crew loaded up the boat and Mistress MacLean prepared her thread, and before they set out she told Donald that when it was dead calm he should release the first knot, then if he needed more wind in his sails, he could loose the second. However, he was on no account to loose the third, because it would whip up a hurricane and he would never get home.

So they rowed out from the shore, letting go one of the knots as they put up the sail. A nice breeze sprung up and pushed them along. At the point where the gale usually blew up against them they loosed the second knot and it sent the boat scudding along towards Barra, almost too fast for comfort, but Donald did not reef the sail because he wanted to be safely home before the witch got up in the morning.

Once inside the loch at Castlebay and nearly home, Donald decided to test what the white witch of Coll had told him, so he untied the third knot. A fierce gust of wind flung his boat right up on the shore – but no harm was done. If he'd loosed the knot out at sea, however, they would all have been drowned.

As Donald walked up to his croft the neighbour came up to welcome him.

'Get out of my sight, woman,' he said, 'you've kept me on Coll since July with your witchcraft. Get your cow off my land and let me never set eyes on you again.'

It's said the lady sold her cow, left the island and was never heard of again.[36]

The white witch in this tale dissolves the black witch's spell by spinning thread and tying knots. Balls of thread, distaffs and spindles turn up time and again in Irish and Scottish stories – remember the way in which the chief woman pulls Bran and his crew into her island in 'The Voyage of Bran'. Fedelm the poet-prophet in the *Tain* carries a 'weaver's beam of white bronze', and then there are the graves in Dorset where middle-aged and elderly women were buried with their heads severed, lower jaws removed and spindle-whorls laid beside them. There are many other tales in the Scottish islands about witches using thread to bind men to them against their will.

Of course, this is not only a Celtic phenomenon. In *Njal's Saga* there is a description of women weaving where 'the heads of men were the weights, but men's bowels the warp and weft, a sword the sley and arrows were the reels'. Then there are the Three Fates of the ancient Greeks – Clotho the spinner, Lachesis the measurer and Atropos the cutter. In the Cretan myth Ariadne saves Theseus from the Minotaur in the labyrinth by means of her 'clew', which is a thread.

In Scotland the distaff came to symbolize the power that women could wield, being used as it was in the female mystery of spinning. It was a three-pronged rod on which you would fix the fleece before you started spinning and was said to 'represent the Holy Trinity'. In Christian times it may well have done, but it also represented the magical Celtic 'three', which symbolizes integrity and 'the creation' (the 'one' symbolizing 'the creator'). It was said that a boy or a male beast should never be struck with the distaff, lest it deprive him of his potency.

The three comes up again in the traditional practices which the women performed when the woven cloth was 'waulked' or finished. While a group of women sat round the cloth tugging and stretching it into shape, there would be three women in charge: the woman of waulking, to make sure the work was done properly; the woman of the songs, to make sure the songs and the singing were good; and a third to make sure no taboos were broken, as would happen if one woman's voice drowned out the others' or a song was sung twice. After the jollity of the work there would be a solemn ceremony to dedicate the cloth in which each member of the household for whom the cloth was intended would be solemnly mentioned by name: 'This cloth for my beloved child Catherine . . .'[19]

# WEAVING AND WITCHCRAFT

Weaving, the creation of cloth by the putting together of threads, is an act of transformational magic in itself, but it is also interesting to think about the state of mind which it might produce in the weaver. It is repetitive work which nevertheless requires great concentration. The weaver cannot 'switch off', like a modern factory worker, because there are too many moments when she must be subtly adjusting the tension, thinking about which thread to bring in, to follow the pattern. I would surmise that long sessions of weaving would put a woman into states similar to those which meditation produces, and that therefore good weavers would have a serenity and an understanding of concepts beyond the everyday. They might come to possess the kind of knowledge which cannot be put into words and which eludes us in our overly busy, workaholic urban lives. These women would certainly arouse awe and respect, which might sometimes turn to fear. And in some cases too they might use their gifts for bad ends. Clearly, this power to weave webs (whether of wool or of the stuff of the psyche) and use threads to attract and draw in is feared by men as much as it is admired or desired, and indeed fear and hatred of witchcraft are very pronounced in many Scottish tales. In one case, when a man discovers that his little daughter and his wife are both witches who can make a ship founder with their spells, he kills them without compunction and nothing is said about it.[37] Among the Barra tales there is an amusing true story told by the 'Coddy', a famous

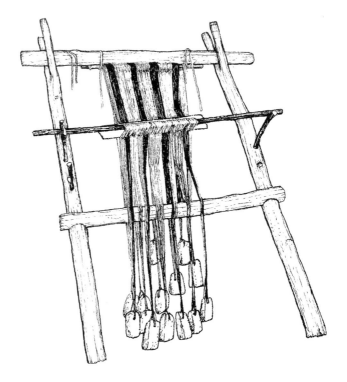

*Weaving loom. Weaving is an act of trans-formational magic in itself.*
(Craig Chapman)

island character, about the time he helped an old lady whose roof was leaking by arranging a visit from the Inspector of the Poor. In gratitude, she wanted to teach him about the *frith*, which was a way of prophesying or divining. She started to explain that you had to get up at daybreak and note exactly what animals were in your field of vision at that time. But the 'Coddy' stopped her in mid-flow; he was worried that he was being taught witchcraft and refused the offer of hearing the secret rhymes you had to say to accompany the *frith*.[33]

Norah Jones reports a neat tale of successful contemporary witchcraft. In a rural part of Ireland in 1991 two youths broke into an old woman's house and robbed her. She could not stop them physically, but put a detailed and eloquent curse on them which so disturbed them that they were forced to return to beg her to lift it – and were caught by the Irish police.[19]

## THE SECOND SIGHT

The 'second sight' of the Highland people is not confined to one sex, although in my own family the tale is of a great-great-grandmother who dreamed of disaster at the pit where her husband worked and persuaded him not to go in the next day, thus saving him from a terrible death when the tunnel roof caved in. Such stories are common in mining communities, and other places where people live with the risk of death.

134

There are fascinating traces of what were probably originally shamanic practices in some old customs concerning women and the sea. Hilda Ellis Davidson tells of an old tradition whereby if a ship failed to return, a certain ritual was carried out. It had to be performed by a woman who was a virgin. She would lie down and go to sleep, and while she slept her spirit left her body and searched for the ship. The woman had to be of strong mind, because if the wind changed while her spirit was absent from her body, she risked losing her reason. When her spirit returned to her body, she woke up and reported where the ship or its wreckage was to be found and what had happened to the people aboard.[38]

Why did the woman have to be a virgin? Possibly because of the idea that intercourse and childbirth weaken a woman by making links with others through which her energy can be leached. A virgin is guarded, a being unto herself, therefore her boundaries are less vulnerable.

There are also accounts of women watching the progress of battles in the sky. A group of women stood on the Bridge of Inverary on 10 May 1773 and watched the battle of Ticonderoga, part of the American War of Independence. They were able to tell which of the soldiers from Argyll had been wounded or killed long before they heard by the mail.[38]

There is one phenomenon which can also affect people who do not usually have 'the sight' or associated gifts, the *seinn-bais* or 'death-music', a high-pitched humming which portends the death of someone connected with the person who hears it. I had a personal experience of this one Saturday afternoon when I sat down after lunch to meditate. All through my half-hour session I experienced a loud metallic ringing in my skull, making it very difficult to carry on. When I switched the TV on afterwards the horrific scenes of the Hillsborough football disaster were being shown. I was working in Liverpool at the time and had (and still have) a deep affection for the place and its (mainly Celtic) inhabitants. It may be I had involuntarily picked up some echo of the dying people's agony.

# THE CAULDRON

The cauldron is one of the central Celtic symbols, particularly associated in the collective psyche with female witches such as Cerridwen. But some would argue that the cauldron actually belongs to the male god, Bran.

Cerridwen is a Welsh version of the Morrigan, a fierce crone-like goddess who possesses a cauldron in which she brews up a mixture which will bring inspiration and knowledge to anyone who tastes it. The substance is intended for her ill-favoured son, Afagddu, but it is in fact the little lad who has been set to stir the cauldron, Gwion Bach, who gets the benefit of it when three drops of the liquor splash on to his finger and he licks them off. Cerridwen pursues him through many shape-changes: he becomes a hare

Right: *Cauldron with
shape-shifting
Cerridwen-Boar.*
(Craig Chapman)

and she a greyhound, and so on. Eventually he turns into a grain of corn,
she into a hen and she eats him. Nine months later he is born as her son and
becomes the great poet Taliesin.[12]

Again in a Welsh tale – the tragic story of *Branwen, Daughter of Llyr*
from *The Mabinogion* – we come across another cauldron belonging to a pair
of unruly giants, who give it to Branwen's brother, Bran, as a gift. This

Opposite: *Cerridwen and
her cauldron.*

cauldron is to be filled with warriors killed in battle, who will then be brought back to life after being boiled up in it, although they will be unable to speak a word.

Hidden in both these stories is the idea that a visit to the land of the dead confers knowledge, a different kind of knowledge, about which it is impossible to speak, except perhaps in poetry, hence Gwion's transformation into a poet. In various cultures we hear of shamans being chopped into little pieces and boiled up in a cauldron, so that they lose their own shape and can take on any shape at will. This shape-changing also happens to little Gwion.

We also know that the Irish bards used to wear cloaks of bird feathers, again suggesting a shamanic origin for their tradition. Bran the Blessed is the patron of bards, and a great singer and tale-teller.

In the tales of both Bran and Cerridwen the cauldron is used as a symbol of transformation and perhaps the cauldron rightly belongs to both of them, reminding us once more of the Celtic insistence on polarity, the tension and power of the opposites. There is no dance of creation without it, after all.

# THE NEW DANCE

The death-bringing goddesses and heroines we've looked at in this chapter hark back to a time before the idea of the individual had taken hold. The hero was only individuated as far as he needed to be in order to act on behalf of the tribe or the community. Therefore death, though terrible, was seen as a gateway through which beings swam as they changed from one form to another. This sense of the unity of all things and the transmigration of souls comes up frequently in Gaelic poetry. The poet Amergin sings:

> I am a wind on the sea,
> I am a wave of the ocean,
> I am the roar of the ocean,
> I am a powerful ox,
> I am a hawk on a cliff,
> I am a salmon in pools,
> I am a lake in a plain,
> I am the strength of art,
> I am a spear with spoils that wages battle,
> I am a man that shapes fire for a head.[39]

With Christianity came the idea of the individual soul, which could be saved through devotion to Christ. Life was no longer an adventure, a terror or a pleasure to be repeated in different forms, but a testing ground, from which, if you did the right things, you could pass into a happy afterlife.

It was during Celtic times that this great polarity between the old form of spirituality, where the ascendancy of the death goddess was accepted, and the new form, headed by Christ the Saviour, who comes to bring eternal life, began to create its tensions and to build up its energy. And we still do not know what the outcome will be. Perhaps a philosophy which includes the truth of both extremes and moves us on to a higher level of understanding. After all, it is said that paradox appears only when we are looking at things with a literal eye, and that when we expand our consciousness it dissolves.

Certainly, for women who want to participate in this renewal, the Celts provide plenty of clues and role models, whether it be Arianrhod and Brigit protecting the holy space of creation, Dana and Rhiannon teaching the knowledge of the Otherworld, or Boudicca and Scathach initiating people into the mysteries of death and rebirth. The women's knowledge which went underground when British Christianity turned its back on female power is lying half hidden, just waiting to be found again.

# 8 MUSES AND MYTH-MAKERS

## *THE DISTAFF OR THE BROOMSTICK?*

As we move from the Iron Age into the Dark and Middle Ages, we begin to find records of real Celtic women, not creatures of myth and legend but historical figures whose existence is undisputed: women like La Duchesse Anne, whose loyalty to her native Brittany was maintained through two marriages with French royalty; like the piratical warrior woman Grace O'Malley, who had an audience with England's Elizabeth I; like the brave and level-headed Flora Macdonald, who saved the life of Bonnie Prince Charlie. As we reach the late nineteenth century, we encounter the women who helped make the 'Celtic Renaissance' in Ireland and Britain, women like the extraordinary Maud Gonne, Augusta Gregory and Constance Markievicz, like Lady Charlotte Guest, the first person to make a readable translation of *The Mabinogion*.

It would be stupid to generalize about the nature of Celtic women in the last 900 years, especially remembering that 'Celt' is not really a racial description but a cultural and linguistic one. However, the women mentioned above do share one fascinating feature: they all in different ways participated in the creation of the seductive Celtic myth, either as translators, collectors and interpreters of the old stories, or by becoming themselves the creatures of myth, partaking in the glamour and power of the great archetypes of queen, warrior woman or priestess. They were not necessarily good or nice or admirable, but they were certainly powerful, and in either large or subtle ways they changed the world.

## *La Duchesse Anne*

In 1488 the defeat of the Breton army at St Aubin-du-Cormier marked the end of Brittany as an independent state. When François II of Brittany died three weeks later the marriage of his young daughter, the 11-year-old Duchesse Anne, became a critical issue.

Matters were complicated by the fact that Anne was already showing herself to be a self-possessed and stubborn young woman, unwilling to be the pawn of forces outside herself. At 13 she gave a spirited address to her ministers of state, saying that she would take the veil rather than marry the immoral old rake Alain d'Albret, who had conceived a violent passion for her. Later, ambushed by his cohorts, who planned to kidnap her and force her to marry him, instead of running away, she turned her horse to face her enemies, rode boldly up to them and reproached them for their disloyalty. They were so awed by her courage that they let her continue on her journey unmolested.

Her first marriage, to Maximilien of Rome, did not last because the two of them never managed to meet, and eventually it was dissolved so that she would be free to marry the king of France, 18-year-old Charles VIII. At first Anne was resolutely opposed to this marriage too, and there are rumours that she was in fact forced into it, the political reasons being that, as queen of France, she would be able to protect the interests of her native Brittany. However, although it may have had an unhappy beginning, the marriage was to blossom into genuine love. Charles allowed her to have her own special guard of 100 Breton gentlemen, who accompanied her wherever she went. Both the French and Breton people loved her because she was young, pleasant-looking (with a slight limp) and good. Her influence helped to clean up the corrupt court and many mothers clamoured to send their daughters to serve her, so high was her reputation.

Sadly, the three sons and one daughter she had with Charles all died in childhood, and her young husband expired from a bump on his head received during a collision with a low archway under which they were passing on their way to watch games. Anne was inconsolable. She wept continuously for two days and nights, refusing to eat or drink, lying prone on the floor of her chamber.

When she recovered, Anne, now 23, wished to devote herself to her beloved Brittany. One of her good works was to arrange for a full and accurate history of the country to be written. But the new king, Louis XII, wanted to marry her; indeed, under the terms of her first marriage, she *had* to marry him, so that the kingdoms of Brittany and France would be firmly yoked together. Unfortunately he already had a wife, the pious Jeanne de France. Louis arranged to have the marriage annulled and Anne agreed to marry him as long as the terms were favourable to Brittany. The people of France were not happy to see their good Jeanne treated like this, but Anne had in fact been in love with Louis in her childhood, so she put aside her own scruples and said yes.

Louis seems to have loved her deeply and left the governance of Brittany to her and her Breton council, calling her affectionately '*ma Bretonne*'. But when their daughter Claude was born, dissent arose between them over whom she should eventually marry. Anne wanted her to marry a relative of her first husband, Maximilien, while Louis, and the people of France, felt she must marry the Duc de Valois, the next heir to the throne, so that once again France and Brittany would be safely joined.

There is a story from her life which is revealing of her darker side. On one occasion King Louis was seriously ill and seemed likely to die. Anne was unpopular at this time, because of her efforts to betroth her daughter to the wrong man, and feared for her safety if the king were to die. So she packed up all her plate and valuables and shipped them to Brittany. To her fury, her ship was intercepted by the Maréchal de Gie and stopped from proceeding. The king recovered but Anne was extremely vindictive in her pursuit of the man who had dared to oppose her, even paying the cost of the prosecution when he was taken to court for lese-majesty. He was very nearly executed, but instead was allowed to live out his life in humiliation and disgrace. Indeed, there is still a saying today attributed to Anne in Brittany which shows her strong and determined character: '*Quic-en-groigne, ainsi sera, car tel est mon bon plaisir*' ('Grumble who may, thus shall it be, for such is my good pleasure').

Her emblem was the ermine, and on one town visit the citizens presented her with a live one, which she took into her arms and cuddled. However, the little beast decided to disappear down the front of her dress. Anne was most discomforted, until one of her ladies wisely said, 'But madam, what do you fear? Is not the ermine your cognizance?'

She lost two more sons in infancy before her second daughter, Renée, was born in 1510. There seems to have been some medical neglect at this, her eighth *accouchement*, and four years later she died of an illness caused by it, aged only 36. Claude did marry the Duc de Valois, who became François I of France when Louis died. He took more interest in the rule of Brittany than Louis had done, but nevertheless the country retained its own culture and Breton flourished as a literary language because of the presence of a half-Breton queen at court.

La Reine-Duchesse Anne is still remembered with affection in Brittany today as a woman of robust character who protected the interests of Breton identity at a critical time.[40]

## Grace O'Malley ('Granuaile')

Grace was born around 1530 on the west coast of Ireland, near Galway, at a time of great turbulence in the struggle between the Irish and the English crown. She came of a seafaring family famous for trading and piracy, her father a Gaelic chieftain under the old Brehon laws.

Grace was tall, dark-haired and dark-complexioned, and at the age of 16 she married Donal O'Flaherty and went to live at his castle of Bunowen. She had two sons and a daughter by him, but seems to have much preferred piracy to motherhood. She took over her husband's raiding operations and made a name for herself attacking the merchant ships which used the port of Galway. She would swoop out of the shelter of the islands in a swift galley and force a lumbering merchantman to a halt. Her men would scramble aboard and she would negotiate with the captain. Booty would either be taken or given and then Grace and her party would disappear swiftly into the mists of Bunowen. She would also sail to Ulster, Scotland, Spain and Portugal to trade local produce and come back with wines, spices, glass, iron, rich silks and fabrics to sell.

Once Grace was besieged in her castle by the English. When conditions were getting really bad inside, she had the idea of melting lead from the roof and tipping it down on to the enemy. The tactic worked, the enemy retreated to the mainland and she dispatched a man after dark to the hill of Doon, from where he lit a beacon which flashed out the message of her plight. Other beacons relayed the news and her allies put to sea, saved her and routed the English.

When her husband was killed by his enemies, she defended their castle against them, but was denied the third of his possessions which the Brehon law allotted to her. So she returned to her father's kingdom and operated with her band of 200 men from there.

On St Brigit's day news came of a vessel which had foundered near Achill Island, so Grace and her men put to sea in a gale, only to find that the ship had broken up. However, Grace came upon one of the young sailors near to death, took him home and nursed him back to health. His name was Hugh de Lacy and they fell in love, but the idyll was not to last long. Hugh was killed by enemies while deer-hunting on Achill. Grace avenged this act by attacking their boats while they were on a pilgrimage to the holy island of Cahir, killed those responsible and took over the stronghold of Doona. One of her titles was the Dark Lady of Doona.

In 1566 Grace married the powerful chief 'Iron Dick Burke', for the period of 'one year certain'. Legend has it that after this year she installed herself in his castle and yelled down to him from the ramparts, 'I dismiss you', taking advantage of the Brehon laws which allow either party the right to divorce the other.

At any rate, her next son, Theobald, was born the next year, possibly on board ship. It is said that she had to appear on deck the day after his birth to give heart to her men under attack. She emptied a blunderbuss at the Turks saying, 'Take this from unconsecrated hands!'

Eventually it seemed politic to Grace to submit to the English and she offered Sir Henry Sidney her services. He noted that she seemed a dominant woman but had a pleasing and 'a most feminine appearance'. Sir Philip Sidney, his son, was captivated by her too.

Once, when returning from a trip, she landed at Howth and went to the lord of the area for hospitality. However, his gates were closed against her and he sent a message that he was at dinner and not to be disturbed. So, Grace then abducted his son and sailed back to Connacht with him, only returning the boy when the Lord of Howth made a vow that his gates would never again be closed against guests. When Anne Chambers, author of a

biography of Grace, visited the Howth residence in recent years, she found that an extra place was laid at table there to this day and was photographed sitting at it.

Grace was outstandingly brave in battle. Once, in the thick of the fighting, her son Tibor tried to hide behind her. 'Are you trying to hide behind my backside, the place that you came from?' she asked, and the shamed boy soon took his place again at her side.

For her various revolts against the English or attacks on other merchant ships, Grace was twice jailed, but in both cases she was released without harm. But by the time she reached the age of 60 she was in a tight spot. Her son Tibor was held hostage by the harsh English governor, Richard Bingham, and then her brother was arrested by him too. She was also very short of money. In a bold move Grace wrote to Elizabeth I, asking the queen to settle on her the maintenance to which she was entitled from her husband's estates and begging to be free to 'invade with sword and fire all your highness's enemies'.

In 1593 she set sail for England and presented herself at court in a chieftain's cloak of green over a yellow bodice and petticoat, her hair gathered on the crown and secured with a silver bodkin. Grace saw the encounter as a meeting of equals – she the queen of Connacht, Elizabeth the queen of England. Elizabeth held her hand high, but Grace was the taller, so the queen had to raise her hand up to meet Grace's. When Grace asked for a handkerchief she was given a delicate lacy one, which she threw on the fire after use, to the queen's amazement. It was then explained to her that in England such things were washed for another day, to which she retorted that she found this a dirty habit.

The queen was impressed. Grace's son and brother were pardoned and Bingham was told to arrange that Grace should receive her share of the inheritance. Grace, however, intended to combine loyalty to Elizabeth with piratical activities to recoup her losses. Bingham thwarted her by quartering large numbers of soldiers on her, thus rendering her penniless. She struggled on, petitioning the treasurer, changing sides as she felt politic, mounting raids as and when she could, and died sometime around 1603.[41]

Cartimandua remains unpopular in Britain, but Grace's pragmatic switching of sides and consorting with the enemy do not seem to have stopped her becoming a national heroine for the Irish, along with Roisin Dubh and Cathleen ni Houlihan. She did what was necessary to survive, was an extraordinarily charismatic leader of men, being tall, fine-looking and charming, as well as astonishingly brave. Whether or not she killed innocent people we don't know. Her rescue of the young sailor Hugh de Lacy suggests she had a kind heart, but she may of course have had ulterior motives. Somehow she captivates us after 400 years, just as she did Elizabeth I, and such moral questions do not seem appropriate in her case.

*Grace O'Malley meets Elizabeth I.*

145

## Flora Macdonald

We expect the Irish Celt to be wild, passionate and feckless, while the Scottish Celt or Gael is usually thought to be a more circumspect character, canny and stalwart and perhaps a little dour. And strangely enough Flora Macdonald seems to fit that description almost exactly.

Born in 1722 on the island of South Uist, she was a small, neat person, taught at home to speak well, without a Scottish accent, as was the custom in her class (upper but not necessarily wealthy), to sing, to sew, to read and write a little. She grew up in an atmosphere of expectation: would there be another attempt by the Jacobites to put a Stuart on the throne? The attempt in 1715 had failed, but now Prince Charles Edward Louis Philip Casimir Stuart, the elder son of James Stuart and Polish princess Clementine Sobieski, was of age. He was a charming, handsome and sincere young man. Andrew Lang wrote that he 'loved the wintry woods . . . hunting, shooting, walking stockingless, all to harden himself for the campaigns which lay before his imagination'.

Scotland was divided. The Campbells under the Duke of Argyll supported the government, while many others still nurtured the dream of their own man on the throne. Flora enters history one midsummer night, when she was staying up alone at her family's shieling (hut) to mind the sheep on their high summer pasture. The full moon was glittering on the Atlantic sea below the slopes, when three fugitives appeared out of the darkness. One was Prince Charles, who had found himself trapped on South Uist by government soldiers. Flora saw a tall young man with dark-red hair and freckles, his face long and sunburnt, his eyes black, his expression thoughtful and melancholy. He had escaped from the battlefield of Culloden, where 1,000 Jacobites had been slaughtered and another 1,000 taken prisoner. Thereafter 'Butcher' Cumberland had laid waste to the land, hanging or bayoneting women and children in revenge, setting fire to farms and livestock.

Flora was asked whether she would help the prince to escape the net which was closing around him. The idea was that he would dress up as her serving woman and together they would cross over to Skye. At first Flora was not enthusiastic. But she gave the three men some cream to drink and then allowed herself to be persuaded.

Soon she and her family were busy making a dress to fit this rather big, ungainly 'girl'. It was a printed linen gown with a white background sprigged with blue and underneath it was a light-coloured quilted petticoat. Over it Charlie would wear an apron and a hooded cloak of dun camlet. His stockings would be held up by a pair of blue garters.

Flora had assented to carry out the ruse, but she insisted on certain terms: Colonel O'Neil was not to come with them, because he did not speak the Gaelic or know the land and would therefore be a liability. The prince was not to bring his pistols; only a cudgel was to be taken for self-defence if necessary.

One night Flora, the prince and one companion slipped into a boat and were rowed by five strong oarsmen out in the direction of Skye. There was a gale, thick mist and heavy rain. The prince insisted that the last half-bottle of

*Flora Macdonald.* (National Gallery of Scotland)

wine be saved for Flora, 'lest she faint with the cold and other inconveniences of a night passage'. He sang Jacobite songs to keep their spirits up, and by morning the rain had stopped and they were close to Vaternish in Skye. There were soldiers out on the rocks watching, so they put into a sea cave and ate breakfast before rowing across to Kilbride in Trotternish.

Later Flora and her companions walked with the prince in his 'Betty Burke' disguise to Kingsburgh House, and it is said that people who saw them were moved to indignation by the free stride and impudent manner of the big 'girl' who swung along with them. The next day the prince headed off over the hills to Portree, while Flora and her companion, MacEachain, went by horseback along the road. When they met up for the last time the prince gave Flora one of his garters and said, 'For all that has happened, I hope, madam, we shall meet at St James's yet and I will reward you there for what you have done.'

He set off for Raasay, and Flora had a few days of liberty before she was arrested. She did her best to protect her friends, but there was little she could do to save them from being rounded up. On Raasay retaliation was vehement: 300 houses were burnt, 32 boats, 280 cows and 700 sheep, but General Campbell gave orders that the self-possessed Miss Macdonald was to be treated with respect, and indeed she was.

On the ship called the *Furnace* in which the Jacobite prisoners were confined, Flora met up with her co-conspirator O'Neil, who told her, 'Only be careful to make your conduct all of a piece. Never once pretend (through an ill-judged excess of caution and prudence) to repent or be ashamed of what you have done.'

The leaders of the rebellion were executed, while Charles Stuart skulked in the heather, waiting for a chance to slip into a boat for France. Flora was brought to Edinburgh, where she became quite a cult with the Jacobite ladies, who admired her gravity, her sweet singing voice and her genteel manners at the tea-table. By the time the prince was safe in Brittany, Flora had been moved to London, where she was nominally a prisoner, though she was given plenty of freedom to visit and receive visitors. A general amnesty in July 1747 set all the remaining Jacobite prisoners free and she returned to Edinburgh to resume her life as an admired celebrity.

After enjoying Edinburgh for a couple of years, Flora married Allan Kingsburgh, son of the man who had sheltered herself and the prince overnight on Skye. She bore seven children and in middle age was visited by Samuel Johnson and his companion Boswell on their tour of the Western Isles. Johnson wrote to his friend Mrs Thrale, 'She . . . is of a pleasing person and elegant behaviour', and having spent the night in the room where the prince had slept, he left behind a note saying, 'With virtue weighed, what worthless trash is gold.'

Flora and her husband had serious financial problems, like many of the Highlanders of the times, and finally emigrated to North Carolina, where

Allan became involved in the War of Independence – on the side of the British government! They were separated for long periods, suffered alarming setbacks, but both survived. Flora returned to the islands in 1779 and died aged 68 in 1790.

Her funeral was the greatest ever seen on the island, with a cortège winding round the hills for a mile, a dozen pipers playing and 300 gallons of whisky drunk at the feasting afterwards. The monument which her son built to her disappeared within months, its slender marble shaft entirely chipped away by Scottish admirers who wanted keepsakes.

Flora was a woman whose quiet, steely courage combined with elegance, down-to-earth shrewdness and integrity to make her a classic heroine, still much loved by the 'dissenting' Scots today.[42]

## Charlotte Guest

It is intriguing that the two bodies of narrative most quoted in this book both received their first accessible and readable translation from women, Charlotte Guest and Augusta Gregory. Moreover, they were women who were not native-speakers of Welsh or Irish and had to master those languages first. The fact that they made these fascinating texts available to a wide public contributed enormously to the Celtic Renaissance of the nineteenth and early twentieth century, and put people back in touch with the originals from which their folklore archetypes had sprung.

Lady Charlotte was born in 1812 and in the course of her long life she was a translator, a businesswoman, a collector, an educator, a mother of ten and an assiduous keeper of a journal. After an unhappy and constricted childhood, she married at 21 an older widower, Josiah Guest, one of the great iron-masters of South Wales. Although English herself, when she went to live in Dowlais near Merthyr Tydfil she fell in love with Wales and was anxious for her children to grow up Welsh and Welsh-speaking. She combined brisk and affectionate motherhood with a ferocious programme of studies, including Arabic and Persian, and only two weeks after the birth of her sixth child she was absorbed in her translations from the Welsh.

Her independence of mind and originality are shown in the fact that she saw long before others the absurdity of ignoring our own traditions in favour of Greek and Latin. She romanticized Wales and, in the manner of the day, bowdlerized some of the robust references to sexual acts, but her translations from *The Red Book of Hergest* (which she turned into *The Mabinogion*) are marvellously evocative of a lost age. She never attempted to diminish the odd, strong convincing magic of the tales and turn it into something familiar and predictable. Her translations, apart from small slips in scholarship, are still among the best we have, models of liveliness and accuracy which have never really been superseded.[43]

149

## *Augusta Gregory*

Born 40 years later, Augusta's life starts off looking remarkably similar to Charlotte's. She too had an unhappy childhood – she was unloved and disparaged by her mother – and married an older man, Sir William Gregory, MP, who was governor of Ceylon. They lived in his family mansion at Coole Park in County Clare, which Augusta made into a sanctuary and talking shop for the makers of the Irish literary Renaissance such as W. B. Yeats, Sean O'Casey and J. B. Synge. Augusta was Irish born and bred herself, her blood a mixture of Celt with the Anglo-Saxon and Huguenot of various invaders, and she witnessed the misery of the poor tenant farmers at close quarters in her childhood. However, she never became a political animal, like Maud Gonne or Constance Markievicz. In fact, apart from an exciting extramarital affair with handsome poet Wilfred Scawen Blunt (which introduced her to 'the joys I was late to understand'), Augusta did not show much individuality until her husband died when she was 40, leaving her a widow with one child.

Now she discovered that the Irish people held hidden riches in the lowly hovels which hitherto she had entered only as a do-gooding charitable lady – here was a vast body of folklore and stories. She began to visit the Irish people, not to patronize them, and found that she liked them and their stories very much – and they liked her. Later in her life the playwright Sean O'Casey wrote of her: 'The taste of rare wine mingled with that of home-made bread on the tip of her tongue: her finely shod feet felt the true warmth of the turf fire and beside its glow she often emptied the sorrows of her own heart into the sorrows of others.'

She met Yeats, began to collect folklore material for him, and together they launched the Irish Literary Theatre, which was to eventually find its home in the famous Abbey Theatre in Dublin.

It was the beginning of a turning away from the cultural values of England and the creation of an independent Irish culture, whether in the form of ancient themes reinterpreted or innovative and provocative plays. It gave the Irish intelligentsia a sense of self-esteem which centuries of English domination had seriously weakened. Augusta looked after the dishevelled Yeats with respectful devotion, keeping his strength up with beef tea and sending him off to his room mornings and evenings to write. He loved Coole and he deeply appreciated Augusta, writing 'she / so changed me that I live / labouring in ecstasy'.

Augusta was probably in love with him, but he was otherwise engaged with the elusive Maud Gonne. However, he and Augusta had a phenomenally creative work partnership, writing together *Cathleen ni Houlihan* (although Augusta never got any credit for this), talking and planning, sorting out the many hitches and irritations that arose while their troupe of actors rehearsed and performed their plays.

In 1902 Augusta published *Cuchulain*, a version of the national epic, and in 1904 *Gods and Fighting Men*, translations and retellings of parts of the Irish vernacular literature written down in the early Middle Ages. She also wrote many plays on Irish themes which were well received at the time. But her most heroic act was to stand out against small-minded nationalists in the great row which surrounded the production of Synge's *Playboy of the Western World*. Many Irish people considered the play a slander on their race, having a hero who was both a parricide and a liar, and there were eruptions of booing and hissing in the audiences. Even so, as an actor described, during the disturbances Augusta 'stood at the door of the green room as calm and collected as Queen Victoria about to open a charity bazaar'.

According to her admirer Sean O'Casey, Augusta was short and stout and sometimes consumed a large number of buns at teatime.

At 60 Augusta ended 20 years of celibacy by having an affair with the glamorous American benefactor John Quinn, who was 18 years her junior, accepting with quiet dignity when the passion soon relapsed back into friendship. She stepped into the breach to play Cathleen ni Houlihan herself in the play, with Maud and Yeats watching critically in the audience, and saw her beloved home, Coole, survive the Troubles, probably because of her personal popularity with the local people. However, her daughter-in-law was in a car which was ambushed by terrorists and some of her companions, including a pregnant woman, were shot down.

She treated the breast cancer which eventually killed her as a minor irritation and died in 1932, aged 80.[44]

## Maud Gonne

In her lifetime Maud Gonne played out all the main Celtic feminine archetypes. For W. B. Yeats she was the muse-priestess to his poetic priest; for the hungry schoolchildren of Dublin and the starving evicted tenants in the countryside she was a nourishing mother. In the republican struggle she campaigned like a ruthless warrior, willing to kill for the cause (although she never did). Above all, for the Irish people, she was 'Cathleen ni Houlihan', the mysterious sorrowing woman who symbolized Ireland. The paradox was that she was not herself Irish, having been born in 1866 in Aldershot, of an English Hampshire father and mother. She had some French blood in her too, and possibly a bit of the Celtic – she certainly hoped so!

However, she did spend much of her childhood in Ireland, brought there by her father, Captain Thomas Gonne, who was a soldier in the British army, serving in what was then a part of the United Kingdom. She lost her mother when she was four, and as a little girl she and her sister Kathleen were allowed to run wild with the local children and to accompany their nanny to the homes of the poor. There they heard the old stories and

*Maud Gonne.*
(National Library of
Ireland)

witnessed the suffering caused by landlords who threw families out into the street if they refused to leave their pitiful hovels so that estates could be enlarged and modernized. At 19 she wrote: 'I saw the plight of the poor people. They were clinging to their bits of furniture. They wandered about looking for a place to spend the night. I could not bear it.'

After her beloved father's death, she tried to make a career for herself in acting, but although she was a very tall, willowy woman with heavy auburn hair and the kind of good looks which made people stare, she had no natural gift for acting and eventually collapsed with a lung haemorrhage and had to give up. She was to be plagued by weak lungs throughout her life.

At 21 she met and fell in love with Lucien Millevoye, a fervent French nationalist who fanned the flames of her budding republicanism and gave her the idea that she could become the 'Irish Jeanne d'Arc'. She was sent as a courier to Tsarist Russia, risking her life with the coolness which was to characterize her actions throughout her life. On another occasion the man who was rowing her back to her ship off the Greek coast tried to kidnap her, but she simply produced a small pistol from her handbag, pointed it at him and ordered him to row her back. He did. The journalist W. T. Stead, who met her in St Petersburg, called her 'one of the most beautiful women in the world'. She certainly enjoyed living dangerously and was increasingly to flout the confining customs of the Victorian world she lived in.

Back in Ireland she began to move in nationalist circles, and was sent off to investigate and publicize conditions in the west of Ireland. She worked with a fury to help the evicted, organizing the building of huts and the setting up of soup kitchens. Her height, her beauty and her ferocious energy all made her appear like a supernatural being; the people of Donegal called her the Woman of the Sidhe, the Fairy Woman.

In 1889 she visited Irish prisoners who were being kept in harsh conditions in Portland prison, and found herself looking them in the eye and telling them when they would be released. The story goes, of course, that she was accurate in every case. At any rate, the incident launched her reputation as a prophet.

She had a son, George, by Millevoye and lived part of the time in Paris. A commentator who watched her on a public occasion noted, 'While speaking the Celtic druidess looked at no one, her great black eyes full of flame.'

Meanwhile, she had met the poet Willie Yeats and he had fallen in love with her. They shared a passion for Ireland and an interest in magic and the occult. As a child she had been haunted by a 'woman in grey', and Willie tried to help her exorcize this spectre, which seemed to be a previous incarnation of Maud as a corrupt priestess and a murderer of children. He wanted to marry her, but she refused. He hoped that her need of him would eventually wear her down. She was initiated into the magical Order of the Golden Dawn, but actually preferred working with Yeats on their own private, sometimes hashish-fuelled psychic sessions, which had the noble aim of building a Castle of Heroes in Ireland and reawakening the ancient myths. Yeats's dream was that he and Maud would be priest and priestess together at Castle Rock on Lough Key. Much of his most beautiful and poignant love poetry was inspired by her.

Yeats had no idea that Maud had a French lover and a child. Indeed, when the little boy died of meningitis, Maud explained her extreme grief by saying she had adopted him. In 1895 her second child by Millevoye was born, this time a girl, christened Iseult. She seems to have been a loving mother to her children, although she said that she had 'a horror and a terror of physical love' and refused to consummate her relationship with Yeats, even when the affair with Millevoye finished. Poor Yeats had to be satisfied with a 'spiritual marriage', which was sincere and intense enough on both sides, but drove him to a pitch of frustration and misery on many occasions.

Maud continued to work for Ireland's independence from Great Britain and during the Boer War engaged in pro-Boer propaganda – and worse. She tried to implement a plan to put bombs disguised as coals into the hold of a troop ship, which would have killed Irish soldiers as well as English. British intelligence thwarted the plan at an early stage, and maybe in later life, when she had ceased to find war exciting and espoused the cause of peace, Maud was glad of that.

She started a women's organization, the Daughters of Erin, to 'combat every English influence' and use up all the female energy that was refused an outlet in the male Irish Literary Society and other nationalist groups. They chose St Brigit as their patron saint, and Maud's cover name was 'Maeve' after Queen Maeve of Connacht (see Chapter 6).

When Queen Victoria visited Dublin, Maud and the 'daughters' organized an alternative treat for the children called the Patriotic Children's Treat. Some 30,000 children were marched through the streets to Clontark Park, where they were given ginger beer and sandwiches, games and dancing and an inspiring address by Maud, urging them never to join with the English forces. Yeats wondered how many of those children would later carry a bomb or a rifle, their passions ignited by Maud's rhetoric. Throughout their long association, he deplored Maud's political side, feeling that it distorted a basically noble nature.

However, he did not stint, with the assistance of Lady Augusta Gregory, to write a play with a central role for her, *Cathleen ni Houlihan*. This told the story of a mysterious woman who appears in a poor cottage one night just before the son of the family is to be married. She persuades him to leave his sweetheart and his farm and follow her. She is, of course, our old friend the 'Sovereignty' of Ireland, the old, poor woman who will become young and strong and beautiful when her lips are kissed by the rightful king – in this case, when the wrongful king, the English king, is expelled from her land. Maud was no great actress but her performance caused a sensation.

A contemporary wrote: 'Those who had the privilege of being present on that occasion will remember it as long as they live. I have never seen an audience so moved.'

Later Yeats worried that his play had inspired certain men to go out and be shot. Certainly it became a rallying cry for Irish nationalism and should perhaps be considered the one really effective magical act which the self-styled priest and priestess performed, much more dynamic than their eccentric occult self-indulgences.

Maud made a disastrous marriage to a nationalist hero, John McBride, by whom she bore a son, Sean. Her husband became a violent drunk and 'assaulted' Maud's young half-sister Eileen (by Maud's father's mistress), who was living with them. Poor Eileen had to be married off to McBride's gentle brother, while Maud arranged a separation from her husband and fought for custody of their son.

One of her biographers, Nancy Cardozo, claims that now Yeats's and Maud's relationship was sexually consummated, but even if it was, it brought them no lasting happiness. Yeats thought that Maud's 'dread' of the physical expression of love had 'probably spoiled all her life, checking natural and instinctive selection, leaving fantastic duties free to take its place'. In his fifties Yeats gave up on Maud, married a much younger woman, Georgie Hyde-Lees, and was, it seems, very happy with her.

Maud did many good works in her middle and later years, setting up school canteens to feed hungry children, working for the prisoners held during the multifarious and bloody Troubles, finding herself imprisoned in Holloway for a while with Constance Markievicz on the pretext of involvement in a German plot and, during the times of the brutalities of the Black and Tans, keeping an open house for the destitute and the wounded. Her son, Sean, was an IRA leader by the time he was 16, but later, like his mother, he renounced violence.

Her courage never diminished. On one occasion she was leading a demonstration which was about to be fired on by a line of young British soldiers. Maud got up on a parapet and 'smiled contempt' at the officer. They gazed at each other for a full minute; she noted he had fine grey eyes and brownish skin, and the order to fire was never given.

In 1948 the Irish Republic was officially proclaimed and Maud lived to see it. When she died in 1953, aged 85, she seemed at peace with the world. Yeats had predeceased her in 1939, but he left a most intriguing — and critical — comment on her life: 'She had to choose (perhaps all women must) between broomstick and distaff and she has chosen the broomstick — I mean the witch's hat.'

Perhaps what he meant was that Maud had chosen to oppose directly what she hated, thus acquiring a hardness and implacability in the service of the cause which froze the warmth and naturalness he had loved in her. Certainly, from her forties onwards, the photos show a cadaverous woman with an unforgiving and fanatic light in her eyes; she looks like a statue, not a woman of flesh and blood. And yet many people told of her kindness and charm and relished the good conversation that flowed at her table. Perhaps she was at least partly 'possessed' by an archetype or archetypes and lost something of her own individual soul – but not all, for when she died some of her last words were, 'I now feel an ineffable joy.'[45]

## Constance Markievicz

From earliest childhood Constance Gore Booth was shaping herself to fit the role of the woman warrior. Born of the Anglo-Irish aristocracy, like Maud, who was just two years older, she loved riding and sailing and the outdoor life. When she was out hunting, it was remarked that she was 'not only fearless but attracted to danger'. However, she also had the ability to embody other ideal forms of femininity. As a girl, wishing to play the fairy godmother to a large, poor rural family, she dressed herself up as a princess in flowing robes, put a hawthorn wreath in her hair and hid fairy lights in it before going with her sister Mabel, dressed as a prince, to knock on the door. They knocked five times, a mystic number. Once let in, she and her sister danced to the tinkling of the 'dangling gadgets' she carried, while the children of the family and their parents watched bewildered and entranced.

Later she studied art in Paris, became a bohemian and married a Polish count, the artist Casimir Markievicz, by whom she had a daughter, Maeve. After her political awakening, she too devoted herself to the Irish nationalist cause, making a bold move in 1909, when she launched the 'Fianna' ('warband'), a tribe of Boy Scouts who did weapons training along with their camping and sing-songs, to fit them to fight against the English oppressor when the time came.

More single-minded and fanatic than Maud, she neglected her daughter (although she loved her), leaving her to be brought up by her grandmother, while Constance ran soup kitchens for striking workers, demonstrated, wrote propaganda and got herself arrested on one occasion for 'throwing dust and particles at the police'. Constance, much more than Maud, thought of herself actually as a soldier and wore the dark-green uniform of the Citizens' Army with pride, her wide hat pinned up on one side with the insignia of the Irish trade union movement, a red hand. On Easter Monday 1916 she participated as a staff-lieutenant in the famous Easter Rising planned by the socialist-nationalist James Connolly.

The revolt started with the take-over of the Dublin General Post Office and although confusion over whether it was to happen at all had drastically lowered the numbers, the small band of nationalists managed to keep the battle with the British up for nearly a week. Several people on both sides were killed, and the pageboy of the University Club claimed to have seen Constance take aim at the window of the club and fire. It later became

*Constance Markievicz.*
(National Library of
Ireland)

157

widely believed that Constance had shot and killed an unarmed policeman, but there is no hard evidence for this. She shot back at snipers certainly, but is known to have intervened to preserve the lives of at least two unarmed men. Her sister's lifelong companion Esther Roper, who knew her well, was convinced that Constance never really shot at anyone.

The night before the surrender Constance had a mystical religious experience and decided she must become a Catholic. The next day she gave up her pistol peaceably but refused to travel in a British army car. 'I will march at the head of my men,' she said. She and the other leaders, such as James Connolly and Patrick Pearse, all expected to be shot, and indeed all the men were. Constance was spared because of her gender and sent to Aylesbury jail. She was there only a few months before a general amnesty released her.

She spent other short periods in jail in the course of the rest of her life and continued to work ceaselessly for Irish freedom. She stood as an MP and was the first woman ever to be elected to Westminster, although she never took her seat, the loyal oath being an absolute stumbling block for her. On one occasion her daughter, Maeve, came to visit her unexpectedly in London and, being sent down to the hotel lounge to find her mother, was unable to recognize her.

Constance died in 1927 at the age of 59 in great weariness of spirit, saying 'sometimes I long for the great peace of the republican plot'.[46]

# WERE THEY TRUE WARRIORS?

When his daughter was born, Yeats prayed that she would 'become a flourishing hidden tree', not a strident warrior like his beloved Maud or the Amazonian Constance. He wrote:

> An intellectual hatred is the worst,
> So let her think opinions are accursed.
> Have I not seen the loveliest woman born
> Out of mouth of Plenty's horn,
> Because of her opinionated mind
> Barter that horn and every good
> By quiet natures understood
> For an old bellows full of angry wind?[47]

As I write, we see on television the grim, set faces of the young Irishwomen on the Sinn Fein committee negotiating with Britain for the 'six counties' of Ulster to become a part of the Republic of Ireland. Ruthlessness and pitilessness are not qualities that men like to see in women, and indeed when they appear in us they tend to be more extreme than in the male sex.

Jung explained this as 'overshadowing by the animus', meaning that when the repressed masculine side of a woman's psyche begins to develop, it can take over rather too forcefully from her female ego, making her dogmatic, aggressive and unyielding. In the same way, an 'anima-dominated' man can be silly, moody and treacherous. It is as if each sex becomes a caricature of the worst attributes of the other. It is interesting that both Maud and Constance shared a dislike of the physical side of sexuality, and that neither had a marriage of any depth or permanence, suggesting that there was much that was unresolved in their psyches.

It is especially ironic that Queen Maeve, who was a model and heroine to both of them, combined her ruthlessness with a voracious leonine sensuality which neither of them chose to copy. But each age takes from myths what it needs and ignores the rest. Now, when we read their stories, we may find their upper-class arrogance offensive, their frigidity unlikeable, their rigid politics either naïve or ludicrous, but we cannot deny that they seem to inhabit a larger, freer world than us, and that their lives display all the power and glamour of the archetypes which ruled them.

# 9 THE LAND OF WOMEN

We are in the middle of yet another Celtic revival. In Scotland, incomers and locals alike are learning Gaelic, and there is even a Gaelic soap on the TV called *Machair*. In Glasgow, the Celtic Connections music festival, with contributions from all over the 'Celtic' world, from Nova Scotia to Galicia, has been a stunning success and looks like becoming an annual event. In Wales, all children at state schools are encouraged to learn Welsh and to speak in Welsh. In both Northern and Southern Ireland there are Irish-speaking schools, Irish-speaking areas and an explosion of enthusiasm for

*Actress Anna Murray in the Gaelic TV soap opera* Machair. (Scottish TV)

traditional dancing and music. People of Celtic origin come from all over the world to learn Gaelic or Irish on special holiday courses. The bookshops of Dublin are full of glossy volumes about the Celts. At the British Museum lectures on the subject seethe with people who feel themselves to be Celts or to have a personal connection with the Celts. Iona has become a place of pilgrimage for seekers from all over the world who believe that they will find here the true spirit of Christianity which has been lost elsewhere.

Throughout the Celtic world women shine: the President of the Irish Republic is a woman, Mary Robinson; the head of Gaelic at Scottish TV is a woman, Rhoda Macdonald; the traditions of Celtic music are being revived and transformed by singers like Emma Christian from the Isle of Man, Talitha Mackenzie from the US but now resident in Scotland, Karen Matheson of Capercaillie; the world of Celtic myth has been marvellously evoked by writers like Pat O'Shea, Evangeline Walton, Marion Campbell and Moyra Caldecott.[48]

But to ascribe mythical qualities or stature to living women is a dangerous notion: after all, many people likened Margaret Thatcher to Boudicca, and whether you consider that an insult or a compliment (to either woman) depends on your politics. You may find in 'Celtic spirituality', as presented by Caitlín Matthews,[49] the magic, mystery and depth you yearn for, or you may find her ideas backward-looking and sentimental – and nothing to do with the Celtic culture which *you* admire.

And to complicate matters further, some scholars are now saying that the 'Celts' never really existed as a separate entity anyway. In a sense, they claim, we have invented them.

If we have invented them, then they clearly stand for something we value very much indeed. The label 'Celtic' sells books, CDs, music festivals and so on like hot cakes nowadays. 'Celtic' music covers a very wide range of material, from the dreamy twilight world of Clannad and Loreena McKennitt – whose PR pictures make her look like a soft-focus Morgan le Fay – through to women like Heather Heywood or Flora McNeil, who keep alive the authentic oral traditions of Scottish song both in English and Gaelic; from the soulful popular singers like Mary Coughlan, whose only claim to the 'Celtic' label is that she is Irish, through to young women like fiddler Catriona MacDonald from Orkney, who is consciously working to bring young people back to their own traditional musical skills. The only thing all these Celtic women have in common is that they are talented.

Yet anyone who absorbs themselves in the old myths and stories, who ponders the fragmentary evidence that history leaves behind, will be left with a vivid and quite specific sense of what Celtic women were like in the olden days. Who can forget the tart words of the Caledonian matron, 'We find it much better to give ourselves openly to the best men, rather than let ourselves be debauched in secret by the vilest, as you Romans do!', Deirdre's magnificent, skull-shattering death, Grace O'Malley's piratical

*Loreena McKennitt.*
(Celtic Connections)

pragmatism, Scathach's consummate skill in the arts of war, Arianrhod's passionate assertion of woman's independence, the integrity of her body? These were women of strength and authority, with an exuberant, swashbuckling energy which could surface in powerful sexual desire or the will to fight against men who tried to enslave or deceive them. Behind them stands the figure of the great Mother Goddess, who was once worshipped in the Celtic lands, and was never entirely usurped by the gods and priests of what Marion Campbell calls the 'New Way'. The question of what legacy they have left us is a tricky one, which should not, I think, be answered by sweeping generalizations or romanticization of the past. Better to consider individual women and ask how they use the female traditions of the past in their present endeavours of self-understanding and self-expression.

In Scotland, Ireland and Wales women are playing a key role in the revival of the Celtic languages. In Wales there are many women writing only or primarily in Welsh – Menna Elfyn, Meg Elis, Gwyneth Lewis, to name but three excellent poets. Meg Bateman was drawn to write poetry in Gaelic although she did not learn that language until university. She discovered that in Scotland women have proved to be the main bearers of the vernacular poetic tradition, because their waulking songs have survived while the men's rowing or reaping verses have all been lost. The cloth-shrinking and stretching sessions lasted about three hours, and as the women rhythmically pounded the cloth, they would make up extempore verse and songs, often humorous and erotic lines about possible suitors, either to be yearned for in glowing words or spurned with sharp satire.

> Young Alasdair, son of the son of Nichol,
> I wish I could bear you a son,
> five or six or seven,
> and proudly would I nurse them;
> I would give breast and knee freely,
> I would raise them aloft in my palm.[50]

Meg was drawn to these poems by their strong images, the 'certain raw way they have of putting emotion . . . a concrete starkness'. Both in her translations of the old songs and in her own poems, Meg carries on the traditions of the old Gaelic women poets, their bold, direct eroticism, which transports us back to a time before gender animosity to a society where the male–female polarity was accepted and relished, not feared. Remember the carrots the girls used to give the men they fancied in the Hebrides at Michaelmas?

It was Meg who put me on to Nuala ni Dhomhnaill, saying that she was not only a fine poet but a big, fine-looking, red-haired woman after the pattern of the Irish heroines and queens. I thought of Fedelm the

163

*Women performers at the forefront of the current Celtic renaissance:* (clockwise from top left) *Karen Matheson from folk-rockers Capercaillie; Mairead ni Mhaonaigh from Altan; Irish instrumentalist Sharon Shannon; and the internationally acclaimed doyennes of Irish music Dolores Keane* (left) *and Mary Black.*
(Dave Peabody)

poet-prophet from the *Tain*, with her red-gold hair and her triple-irised eyes. 'She's a clairvoyant too,' Meg said, though Nuala denied it when I asked her.

'My sister is though,' she told me. 'She can tell what the exam papers will be the next day, and my mother can see death coming . . . or smell it – a cold-clay kind of smell it is, she says. But I don't feel my job is so much to *see* as to create the patterns of words and sounds to make a presence appear, to call up the muse, to weave a web of words.'

Nuala has chosen to write poetry only in Irish, stating, 'My only, ultimate allegiance is to the Irish language, then to poetry and to my life experience as a woman.' She sees herself as part of a line of *banfhile* (women poets) which includes all the women keeners who made up elegies for the dead, whose poetry was almost never written down and has therefore been wiped out, erased from the male-defined canon. Outside this oral tradition, she says, women were 'denied access to the ink' by the self-protective male caste of bards. In revenge she uses her poetry to ridicule the pervasive myths of Ireland as a sorrowing beautiful woman, by imagining the country as a beautiful naked man! Because she is such a good poet, the poem moves and enchants as well as making its political point:

### Island

Your nude body is an island
asprawl on the ocean bed. How
beautiful your limbs, spread-
eagled under seagulls' wings.[51]

Nuala says of Ireland:

> *Emotionally*, women run this country, but not the institutions . . . You see, we had these institutions plonked down on us and there haven't yet been institutions developed to fit the psyche of the nation. But Mary Robinson is just the start, and I don't see the president of Ireland being a man ever again . . . There was a 100 per cent increase of women deputies elected in the last election and Mary Robinson is a very clever woman. She knows that you can affect the collective unconscious by pushing certain symbols. You don't have to spell out what they mean . . .

Nuala's poetry is infused with imagery from the old tales yet there is nothing sentimental or nostalgic in the tone of her work. The tenderness and candour of her erotic poems strikes the same kind of note as the Scottish waulking verses, something unselfconscious from 'before the Fall', before the time when Christians made women feel ashamed of their bodies and their power over men.

*Mary Robinson, President of the Republic of Ireland.* (Popperfoto)

166

### Blodewedd

At the least touch of your fingertips
I break into blossom,
my whole chemical composition
transformed.
I sprawl like a grassy meadow
fragrant in the sun;
at the brush of your palm, all my herbs
and spices spill open . . .[51]

Of course, if we could read it in Irish who knows what other notes we
would hear, what scents we would detect . . .

For Nuala, the clairvoyant, prophetic side of the poet's role is in
abeyance. For Marion Campbell, it welled up almost against her will and
expressed itself in the writing of her astonishing novel set in ancient
Scotland, *The Dark Twin*. She wrote of the experience:

> This book evolved at a time of deep anxiety and physical exhaustion, out of
> a series of brief waking dreams. Usually, when I am writing children's
> adventure stories, I surround myself with timetables and factual notes; with
> this one, I floundered through the debris of a cutting-room floor from which
> there coiled up fragments of scenes and snatches of unintelligible dialogue.
> I was forced to make notes in order to get rid of these bewildering odds and
> ends; only after I had gathered a pile of loose-leaf pages could I be sure that
> the episodes had any connection.[52]

*The Dark Twin* tells of the period of time when the 'Old Way', in which the
Goddess was honoured and women's power held sway, is challenged by the
'New Way' of the male priests and male gods. It gives us a direct and vivid
glimpse into the world of which the Irish and Welsh narratives are but a
dim remembrance. Here the book's hero, Drust, writes about the three feasts
which the followers of the Old Way celebrated, and you might find the
three goddesses or priestesses associated with them sounding familiar.

> The spring dancing was the time of the Maiden; Mistress of the Gates,
> Queen of Skills, they hailed her. This is she whom I now know to be the
> core of the faith, the vision of life-in-death, the ultimate unobtainable joy of
> poets, on whom to meditate is the beginning of wisdom, on whom to
> presume to think is the beginning of madness. The harvest, my Mother's
> time, was the rejoicing of children, the casting off of age and sorrow and
> the return of joy; the Old One was honoured in winter, with what rites it is
> not meet for a man to know.
>
> These three are so interwoven in symbol and action that mortal thought

may not divide them: the three beasts, roe, mare and sow; the three birds, cuckoo, swan and raven; the colours of silver, blue and red – these are each and all matters a lifetime's thinking cannot plumb.[48]

In this book we have known these three figures under many different names, but perhaps they can all be seen as variations on the central archetypes of Arianrhod, the Lady of Light, Dana, the Lady of the Waters and old Morgan, the Lady of the Underworld. But again, with a true Celtic appreciation of polarity, of the interdependence of male and female, Marion Campbell does not exalt the female at the expense of the male, as later feminist writers have tended to do, bearing witness to the fact that Celtic women do not on the whole fear men. The matriarchal pride still burns strong, the Great Mother may not be insulted or outraged without paying a grave penalty, and this knowledge gives Celtic women a secret inner confidence.

And makes men respect them. The BBC Scotland comedy series *Rab C. Nesbitt* brought a new variety of bitter, black, highly verbal satire to the screen, but running through the coruscating script you will notice an odd cross-current: in the poignant portrayal of 'Mary-doll', Rab's long-suffering wife, by Elaine C. Smith, there is a kind of subtle awe and respect for women you do not find in English comedy series. The women are satirized, of course, along with the men, but with much less savagery. It is as if the writer, Ian Pattinson, to whom, as a true satirist, very little is sacred, draws the line at being too vicious about women. Does he unconsciously fear the revenge of the Goddess, as the men of Ulster had reason to once they had forced pregnant Macha to run the race?

A recent *After Dark* programme on Channel Four about the Catholic Church in Ireland had three female contributors, a nun and two journalists from opposing ideological camps, along with five or six men. The women dominated the programme, verbally and morally, for two hours, and the men sat back and let them do it. I am not sure that women born into the Anglo-Saxon culture would have had the confidence and nerve to do that, without fearing to appear overassertive in their efforts to win their 'rights'.

The poet Rilke had a vision which has bearing on the nature and evolution of the Celtic woman:

Some day there will be girls and women whose name will not merely signify the opposite of the masculine, but something in itself, not of any complement and limit, but only of life and existence: the feminine human being.

The key phrase is 'the feminine human being', the idea being that a woman can exist in and for herself, not only in relation to men and children; that she can be complete within herself, embodying the 'tension of the opposites', the polarity which exists in all really 'human' beings. The 'complete woman', 'the feminine human being' was already trying to be born, to enter history, at the time of the old stories, whether in the shape of quarrelsome Arianrhod or campaigning Ronnat, or the independent female poets and prophets and warriors who have walk-on parts in many of the tales. Here she is, in a glowing celebratory incarnation, in a wedding song collected by Alexander Carmichael in the Scottish Highlands in the nineteenth century:

Dark is yonder town,
Dark are those therein;
You are the brown swan,
Going in among them.

Their hearts are in your controlling,
Their tongues are beneath your sole,
Nor will they ever utter a word
To give you any offence.

A shade are you in the heat,
A shelter are you in the cold,
Eyes you are to the blind,
A staff are you to the pilgrim,
An island are you in the sea,
A fortress are you on land,
A well are you in the desert,
Health are you to the ailing.

Yours is the skill of the Fairy Woman,
Yours is the virtue of Brigit the serene,
Yours is the faith of Mary the gentle,
Yours is the tact of the women of Greece,
Yours is the loveliness of Emer the Beauty,
Yours is the tenderness of Darthula the delightful,
Yours is the courage of Maeve the battler,
Yours is the charm of the mouth of Melody.

You are the joy of all joyous things,
You are the light of the beam of the sun,
You are the door of the chief of hospitality,
You are the surpassing star of guidance,
You are the step of the deer on the hill,
You are the step of the steed on the strath,
You are the shape of the swan of swimming,
You are the grace of all lovely graces.

170

The pure likeness of the Lord
Is in your face,
The loveliest likeness that
Was ever on this earth . . . [11]

The note sounded by these lines is both strong and sweet; it gains its power
from both Christian and pagan sources; its resonances are deep. It is not a
note we hear often in the modern world where our sense of the holy and the
sacred has been thoroughly diminished. I have tried to suggest in this book
that in the Celtic tradition, which took over much from the
Goddess-respecting people who came before the Celts, women had a special
role. They embodied a living connection with that holy inner world,
whether as its guardians, its messengers or indeed its inhabitants, and by
doing so they protected the integrity of all creation. The instructions for
reaching that world can be heard as clearly today as they could be back in
the Dark Ages, in the words of the Otherworld woman to Bran at the start
of his sea journey:

Do not fall on a bed of sloth,
Let not thy intoxication overcome thee;
Begin a voyage across the clear sea,
If perchance thou mayst reach the land of women . . . [1]

# REFERENCES

Numbers within the text refer to the works listed below.

1  T. P. Cross and C. H. Slover, trans. 'The Voyage of Bran' in *Ancient Irish Tales* Holt, Dublin 1936.
2  P. B. E. Ellis *The Druids* Constable, London 1994.
3  S. James *Exploring the World of the Celts* Thames & Hudson, London 1993.
4  Information from Butser Ancient Farm in Hampshire, tel: 01705 598838.
5  P. W. Joyce *A Social History of Ancient Ireland* 2 vols., Longmans, London 1903.
6  Marian McNeill *The Silver Bough* vol. 11, MacLellan, Glasgow 1957.
7  Kuno Meyer, ed. *Cain Adamnan: An Old Irish Treatise on the Law of Adamnan* Oxford 1905.
8  Isabel Henderson 'The Problem of the Picts' in *Who are the Scots?* BBC Books, London 1971.
9  Thomas Kinsella *The Tain* Oxford University Press, Oxford 1970.
10  Dr Daithi O'hOgain *Myth, Legend and Romance: An Encyclopaedia of the Irish Folk Tradition* Prentice Hall, New York 1991.
11  Alexander Carmichael *Carmina Gadelica* Floris Books, Edinburgh 1994.
12  Gwyn and Thomas Jones, trans. *The Mabinogion* Dent, London 1978. See also Lady Charlotte Guest's translation, Dent, London 1937.
13  Bani Shorter *An Image Darkly Forming* Routledge & Kegan Paul, London 1987.
14  Rosalind Clarke *The Great Queens* Colin Smythe, London 1991.
15  Moyra Caldecott *Women in Celtic Myth* Deep Books, London 1995.
16  Miranda Green *The Gods of the Celts* Alan Sutton, Gloucester 1986.
17  Carlos Castaneda *The Art of Dreaming* Aquarian Press, London 1993.
18  Alan Ereira *The Heart of the World* Cape, London 1990.
19  Norah Jones *Power of Raven, Wisdom of Serpent: Celtic Women's Spirituality* Floris, Edinburgh 1994.
20  Lisa Bitel *Isle of the Saints* Cornell University Press, New York 1990.
21  Barbara Walker *The Woman's Encyclopaedia of Myths and Secrets* Harper & Row, New York 1983.
22  Esther Harding *Women's Mysteries* Rider, London 1977.

23  Mary Condren *The Serpent and the Goddess* HarperCollins, New York 1989.

24  John Matthews *Boadicea, Queen of the Celts* Firebird, Poole 1988.

25  Antonia Fraser *Boadicea's Chariot: The Warrior Queens* Weidenfeld & Nicolson, London 1988.

26  Showell Styles *Welsh Walks and Legends* Grafton, London 1988.

27  Juliette Wood 'The Fairy Bride Legend in Wales' in *Folklore*, vol. 103, 1992.

28  Geoffrey Grigson, ed. *The Penguin Book of Ballads* Penguin, Harmondsworth 1975.

29  F. M. Luzel *Celtic Folk Tales from Armorica* Llanerch Enterprises, Lampeter 1985.

30  This version is based on Thomas Kinsella's translation of the *Tain*, see 9.

31  Robert Graves *The White Goddess* Faber & Faber, London 1988.

32  *Folklore, Myths and Legends of Britain* Reader's Digest, London 1973.

33  S. Ritchie and M. Harman, eds. *Exploring Scotland's Heritage: Argyll and the Western Isles* HMSO, Edinburgh 1985.

34  W. Y. Evans Wentz, *The Fairy Faith in Celtic Countries* Colin Smythe, London 1981.

35  Alwyn and Brinsley Rees *Celtic Heritage* Thames & Hudson, London 1978.

36  J. L. Campbell, ed. *Tales from Barra Told by the Coddy* Morris and Gibb, Edinburgh 1975.

37  Rev. Peter Youngson, ed. *Ancient Hebridean Tales of Jura* Peter Youngson Publications, Kirremuir.

38  Hilda Ellis Davidson *The Seer* John Donald, Edinburgh 1989.

39  T. P. Cross and C. H. Slover, see 1.

40  Louisa S. Costello *Memoirs of Anne, Duchess of Brittany, Twice Queen of France* Cash, London 1855.

41  Anne Chambers *Granuaile: The Life and Times of Grace O'Malley 1530–1603* Wolfhound Press, Dublin 1979.

42  Elizabeth G. Vining *Flora Macdonald in the Highlands and America* Geoffrey Bles, London 1967.

43  R. Guest and A. V. John *Lady Charlotte: A Biography of the Nineteenth Century* Weidenfeld & Nicolson, London 1989.

44  Mary Lou Kohfeldt *Lady Gregory – the Woman behind the Irish Renaissance* André Deutsch, London 1985.

45  Nancy Cardozo *Lucky Eyes and a High Heart* Victor Gollancz, London 1979.

46  Anne Marreco *The Rebel Countess: The Life and Times of Constance Markievicz* Weidenfeld & Nicolson, London 1967.

47  W. B. Yeats From 'A Prayer for My Daughter' in *Collected Poems* Macmillan, London 1983.

48 Pat O'Shea *The Hounds of the Morrigan* Puffin, Harmondsworth 1987; Evangeline Walton *The Children of Llyr* Pan, London 1972; Marion Campbell *The Dark Twin* Turnstone, London 1973; Moyra Caldecott, see 15.

49 Caitlín Matthews *The Celtic Tradition* Element, Dorset 1989.

50 James Ross 'A Classification of Gaelic Folk Song', in *Scottish Studies* vol. 1, 1957.

51 Nuala ni Dhomhnaill *Pharaoh's Daughter* Gallery Books, Loughcrew 1990.

52 From the Afterword to *The Dark Twin*, see 48.

# INDEX